"We need never be ashamed of our tears."

- Charles Dickens, Great Expectations.

A Town Of
Mabel's

How I remember
what my Mother doesn't

Christie Wood

BALBOA.
PRESS

A DIVISION OF HAY HOUSE

Balboa Press books may be ordered through booksellers or by contacting:

Balboa Press
A Division of Hay House
1663 Liberty Drive
Bloomington, IN 47403
www.balboapress.com
1-(877) 407-4847

Because of the dynamic nature of the Internet, any web addresses or
links contained in this book may have changed since publication and
may no longer be valid. The views expressed in this work are solely those
of the author and do not necessarily reflect the views of the publisher,
and the publisher hereby disclaims any responsibility for them.

The author of this book does not dispense medical advice or prescribe the use
of any technique as a form of treatment for physical, emotional, or medical
problems without the advice of a physician, either directly or indirectly. The
intent of the author is only to offer information of a general nature to help you
in your quest for emotional and spiritual well-being. In the event you use any
of the information in this book for yourself, which is your constitutional right,
the author and the publisher assume no responsibility for your actions.

ISBN: 978-1-4525-7524-7 (sc)
ISBN: 978-1-4525-7525-4 (e)

Printed in the United States of America.

Balboa Press rev. date: 09/10/2013

For my Grandma, sister and daughter who have taught me how to laugh through adversity, and for Margaret who taught me everything else.

Preface

I started to write a book about my mother. It morphed into a search for answers. Why her? Why this disease? It became a book about my mother with a disease and how I handled it with tenacious determination to always approach her with a smile, willing to meet her wherever she was in that moment.

Chapter One

A cut crystal vase of garden red roses sat precariously on the chipped, green windowsill in my Aunt Mildred's kitchen. It temporally blocked my view of the old man with the Caribbean blue eyes walking toward me. My mind raced as I reached to lock the kitchen screen door with my dish soap-drenched hand. But I wasn't in the city where I lived. I was in the small town of my birth. No one had locks on screen doors here. He was shabbily dressed and wore an old, once-dapper hat. His blue eyes danced beneath the hat. He was skinny with a tanned face like worn leather. I felt panic, yet a sense of calm seemed to be slowly creeping over me. He seemed to be trespassing, actually trampling a few vegetable plants in his self-made path; however, he was familiar to me in some way that I could not understand. I had certainly never seen this man before here or in the city. His journey across the garden, towards the screen door, seemed suspended in time. By the time I realized that I needed a towel, to stop the soapy puddle forming on my aunt's linoleum, he was opening the craggy old screen door.

I was a young girl, not quite a preteen, not quite a child. I knew bad things happened in the world, I knew people kept secrets. What I didn't know was that I had a living grandfather with beautiful blue eyes. As he brushed past me with a wink and a nod, I was paralyzed. As the dishes lay in their porcelain bubble bath awaiting my return, I stood mesmerized, watching an exchange between my aunt and this magic man. I don't remember the words exchanged now, and I couldn't have told you them then. I only saw him as if nothing else in the room had any edges. My eyes fell onto his hands as he accepted cash my aunt pulled from her small coin purse, which she snapped open between her thumb and forefinger without a sound. She snapped it closed again. Only then did it make an audible clicking sound . . .

His hands looked soft, not like his face, which had seen too much sun or life. Knowing what I came to know in the years after this meeting, it was both. As this mystical garden man walked toward the screen door to exit, I fell into his eyes. He winked once again and stopped to turn back toward my aunt with a slight turn from his neck, she simply said to him without prompting, "She's Margaret's youngest girl." He smiled and told me I was just as pretty as my mother. How in the world did this man know my mother? My mother lived far from here, especially if you figure this guy didn't have a car. Or else why wouldn't he have arrived by the front door after he exited it from the curb or driveway?

Once he had departed, I stood perfectly still and silent, awaiting my aunt's explanation in a kitchen that seemed to have just lost an enormous amount of energy. "Christie," she began, "that was your grandfather." You know those sentences that you never thought you would hear? This was one of them for me. I didn't have a grandfather. I had a grandmother, an amazing woman who managed to raise four kids on her own, with a steady job in a cigar factory and the help of The Salvation Army. Mildred, in whose kitchen I now stood, Dorothy, who lived nearby, Margaret, my mother, and Uncle Joe, who was also a resident of this town, I was now finding out I knew nothing about.

This was my mother's family. My father, William (Bill), who was also from this town, had three sisters and no parents. I suddenly realized the whole lot of them could have been raised by wolves for all I knew. I spent that night with Aunt Mildred and Uncle Leo as had been the plan. Restless and full of curiosity I tried to get her long-haired, black-and-white cat to sleep with me to ease my anxiety, but it seemed much more interested in spending the evening outside. My cousins, a son and daughter, teenagers, were off with friends for the evening. Needless to say I could not sleep. Garden sugar peas and blue eyes were dancing in my head. I didn't ask any more questions of my aunt, but I had plenty for my mother come my morning, which could not come fast enough. Little did I know what can of worms I was about to open up for my parents.

My dad and my mom picked me up, not the next morning, but later in the day, after my dad's work I supposed. I rode in the backseat, gathering up the pillow and blanket that were always present on trips between Columbus and Newark. I would prepare my future bed in the back window of whichever Chevrolet my father had that year long before I climbed up into it. It was a time before seat belts and before light pollution stole all of the Milky Way and most of the stars. On the back country roads away from the towns and the cities, you could see the twinkling of the dippers and some guy with an arrow pointed away from you as if to protect us all in our galaxy. My sister, Brenda, was married shortly after high school; we were sixteen years apart, so she was never with us on these trips back to where she had grown up. The youngest boy in our family, Billy, joined us a lot, but he was home for this short trip of my parents, presumably out of harm's way with the oldest boy, Tom. I loved this ride. I was intuitive. I didn't mention my grandfather's visit. I was alone with my mom and my dad and the protector of the galaxy. I stayed quiet. I was at peace.

The gravel of our driveway, the jingle of my mother's keys, and the closing of the ashtray to contain a cigarette that my mother would never admit she had smoked woke me up. My father would retrieve me from my sky bed, and we would both pretend that I was still asleep as he carried me to my bed and covered me along with my attached car blanket. My questions would have to wait until morning or longer. I was feeling anxious about bringing up my grandfather to my mom. I wanted her to understand the magic of the encounter, but something told me this wasn't going to be the case. My mother rarely understood magic.

Days went by before I felt that I had the courage to bring up the subject of my recent encounter with a miracle. The longer I waited in panic, the more I believed this blue-eyed, gentle creature to be a mystical being. I wasn't even sure I had really seen him. After all he didn't have a car for God's sake; everyone I knew had a car. He walked through a garden, trampling plants. Strangely when I later checked, these plants were not trampled at all. And above all else, no one had eyes like that! My mom like every other woman was in love with Paul Newman, a movie star that had beautiful blue eyes, but I had never seen him in real life. This episode was my first awareness of a lifelong habit of holding in anything important to me only to have it explode out of me at entirely the wrong moment. I just wanted it to be understood for what it was to me. I had to plan this carefully. The dinner table was noisy the night my mom said, "I heard that your met your grandfather?" Met my grandfather? I had not met him. I had had a magical experience at which time I found out that a lovely, harmless, beautiful creature was a grandfather that I had previously not known I had. "Did I have any questions?" she wanted to know.

"Just one," I answered. "Why did you not tell me this?"

"What do you mean?" was her reply to that. Now I was no longer full of panic, just confused.

I will be the first to admit that I was a very naïve kid. After all I really thought that there was an extraordinary amount of barmaids named Mabel behind the bars that my father sat me at, sometimes on phone books, sometimes on my knees. Mom was not to know of all of these Mabels, the phone books, or the places where this *special time* of ours took place. That was okay by me. I drank lots of Shirley Temples, a yummy concoction of 7UP, something red, sticky, and sweet, and a bright red cherry or two that I didn't like but always had to have floating on the top of a very tall, thin glass that seemed made for my small hands.

I met a lot of Mabels before I found out the Santa news. And just like the fact that I didn't put two and two together with the abundance of Santas everywhere, all looking basically alike (this is why parents of color go along with the white guy as Santa), I didn't put two and two together with a commercial on television for Black Label beer. A couple of guys were sitting at a bar, and one guy raised his hand for Mabel to bring more Black Label. "Hey, Mabel, more Black Labels." Anyone can do anything to children—television, criminals, schools, parents. The power to brainwash is in every adult. That's all we are—a bunch of brainwashed beings walking the earth trying to sort out the secrets and lies from the truth. For me personally finding out the Santa news was the first time I ever entertained the thought that maybe everything my parents told me was not truth.

It's hard to remember how many times I ended up on a barstool, keeping my dad's secret. It's even harder to remember why. My mom started telling stories about her childhood after the cat was out of the bag that she had had a father. One story was a shared one with my uncle Joe, and when they told it together, it was delightful. Apparently my grandfather was a barber, quite a good one . . . when he showed up to barber. The story goes that Grandfather Ed was supposed to be watching the two younger kids, Margaret and Joe. He took them to work with him, telling them to be good in the barbershop that he would be "right back." That didn't happen, and kids being curious and bored decided to imitate their dad's work. As the older one, Margaret put little Joe in the barber chair, whisked a sheet-looking thing around his neck, loaded him up with shaving cream, and found the straight razor she had seen used for shaving. She was just about to proceed with the unnecessary shaving when an unknown person or persons came into save little Joe. Joe and Margaret were sworn to secrecy by these angels and later the barber himself. Word did somehow leak out though because Ed the barber was never trusted with the care of the two younger children again. I was never saved by any such angels and always kept my father's and my secret. That may be because angels see no need to save little children from spending time with their loving fathers while they drink delicious libations. What angels may not understand though is that kids keeping secrets, regardless of the content, leads to many issues later in life.

I never understood why my mother would get so very upset with my father's drinking. He never seemed drunk to me, except twice a year at Christmas. This was when she would get upset. Every year my father's work would hold a company Christmas party. The arguing would start as my father was preparing to go to this party. She would insist that he did not need to participate in this ritual and that we didn't need the stinking company's turkey gift that he would return home with. He would calmly continue to dress, while he calmly explained the size of the turkey he would return with, as if he was going out on a hunt for the bird. He would head for the door, the tips of his fingers retrieving his fedora from the hat rack. He would lean in to kiss her on the cheek while he placed it on his head in one motion that was so dismissive it appeared cool. My mother's cheek was still in motion as part of the moving apparatus, yelling at him to stay home just one goddamn year.

At the time I didn't get it from her point of view. The man worked hard. He just wanted to go out once a year and get this bird that gets larger every year, and he couldn't possibly miss what might be the biggest bird yet. She finally got smart one year and bought the bird ahead of time, proudly showing my dad that there was no need for his attendance at the hunt. That of course was when it hit me. It wasn't about the turkey. It did not change my opinion that he should go to his company party. But I did tend to wonder why he couldn't just miss one goddamn party since it was after all always held on Christmas Eve, a detail I didn't understand until I had my own family. He always came home drunk.

My dad was a fun drunk. And my uncles were fun drunks as far as I knew. And there was nothing more fun than the family Christmas party with fun drunks. I looked forward to this festivity all year long; it was the only highlight of the season after I had found out about the Santa conspiracy. The evening would begin with my mother's lecture about *not* getting drunk. There was never any mention of the driving part of this. We always took those back roads when drinking was involved under the guise of the saying, "Let's make this night an adventure." The party was always a huge success from my point of view. Everyone had a great time. Nothing was more fun than sneaking downstairs to peak at the men folk playing cards, smoking cigars, and drinking an unbelievable amount of beers. This is also where my cousin and I, as we lay peeking through the rungs of the stairs, that we thought disguised us heard our first dirty joke. A priest and a nun were lost in the desert; it was hot, very hot. They had long ago run out of water. The camel they had been riding had fallen over dead. The priest told the nun they were going to have to take off their garb to survive—she her black, long, and cumbersome habit and he his black and cumbersome *priest outfit*. (We were not Catholic, and my uncle could not come up with the name of what a priest wore, nor could anyone else present.) So the nun began to remove her habit and the priest his clothes. As the priest removed his pants, exposing his *dick*, the nun gasped and asked, "Why, Father, what is that?"

The priest said, "Why, Sister, with this I make life."

To which the nun replied, "Well then stick it in that goddamn camel and let's get the hell out of here!" You never forget your first dirty joke, at least not if it's that good.

The ride home was always brutal with my mom crying and intermittently yelling. This would be when I wanted to tell my secret. He would be telling her that he only drank once a year. "What's the big deal?" he would ask. I believed him. The beers I brought him nightly, the barstools I sat on while every Mabel brought him beers, and the beer ever-present in his hand while he relaxed in his lawn chair aside, he only got *drunk* in December *once a year*; therefore, he drank once a year. I wanted to save my mom . . . always. I wanted her to understand that I was safe, we were all safe, nothing happened, nothing would happen. I was with him a lot when he drank all year long, and he was fine. Nothing bad ever happened. The presence of my grandfather at the family Christmas party, the year after that walk through the garden, changed everything for me. My mother could no longer hold in her painful childhood.

Margaret was only a child when she first experienced *the field*. Grandpa Ed had to watch her the day she was sick and couldn't go to school. Ed needed a drink, needed it badly. There was nothing in the house. Of course, Grandma Mary would never allow that. He couldn't take her to the town square to any one of the bars or stores or anywhere for that matter where he might be seen by any of Grandma Mary's friends, acquaintances, or neighbors with little Margaret in tow. But he could score at the field, a place near the train tracks and far from any *respectable folks*, where the booze flowed freely and the hobos set up camp. Grandpa held Margaret's hand all the way to the edge of the field. Her mind raced with excitement. He told her they were going on an adventure and she would have to be brave. As the Queen Ann's Lace began to reach heights much taller than she was, the train whistle grew louder, and men wearing rumpled clothing and smelling of things dead casually stumbled by, Ed told Margaret to sit very still, be very quiet, and hide amongst the overgrown weeds until he returned. But like the day at the barbershop, he did not return, not until Margaret was alone in the dark after the cold set in and the voices around her had grown loud and crude. In this field there were no angels. The fear and the abandonment were unbearable; however, he had told her to be brave, and that is what she would have to be.

Chapter Two

Margaret wanted another baby. She was past thirty years old and that was ancient in 1953 to be pregnant with child; however, this would be her fourth child, which was much more acceptable.

She broke the news of her pregnancy to Bill shortly after his treatment for depression had been issued in his doctor's office. Bill had missed a day of work simply because he could not get out of bed. Not only had this feeling of immobility never occurred in his life before, but he had certainly never missed a day of work. He had supported himself since he has been thirteen years old, delivering telegrams for Western Union by bicycle. He had moved on to an automobile, another job, and a wife and three children to support. Bill and Margaret had weathered poverty, the Great Depression, Polio and war. Things were going well for them in 1953, so why was he depressed? He had no answers; the doctor's answer came from the bottom locked drawer of his oversized oak desk. The doctor said that Bill just have a sip of whiskey whenever he "felt down." He offered Bill a sip of his own remedy from this drawer.

I was born on a cold December day as the Newark town clock was striking 7:00 a.m. Margaret said she heard the clock. She wanted another girl. The doctor announced she had had a healthy baby boy because of the fact that I weighed in at ten pounds and ten ounces and looked right up to a certain point like a boy. He had barely gotten the word boy out when he had to switch mid announcement to *girl*. She would name me Christie Lee, and by God no one would stop her this time. Christie was to have been her firstborn's name sixteen years earlier, but Bill's sister, Mary, had proclaimed in front of all relatives and friends at Margaret's baby shower that that was a horrible name. Mary was a teacher. She had been to college. Margaret had dropped out of school in the ninth grade because of a lack of shoes, which was fine for the autumn, but Mildred and Dorothy had not yet grown out of their shoes for hand-me-downs for Margaret come winter. Thirteen-year-old Margaret was already wearing a coat from the previous year that had been gifted to her by her teacher. The days were getting colder, and wearing no shoes was just too embarrassing. It wasn't that no shoes were weird. Lots of kids came to school barefoot, but not as the trees turned bare and the skies gray with the promise of snow. Margaret never got over feeling uneducated, and if her educated sister-in-law said Christie was a horrible name, then it must be so.

"I was standing on the playground, alone and shivering when Miss Parkins saw me." This was how my mom would begin to tell me the story of how she acquired her first real winter coat. "It was too big for me, of course . . . but I loved that coat."

She would have this faraway look in her eye whenever she began this story. The first time I heard it, I had no idea what was too big for her until she said the part about loving the coat. After that I would wait patiently for the "I loved that coat" part because that is when the tears formed in her deep-set hazel eyes. She would stay that way for what seemed like an hour when I was a child to shorten only to ten minutes by my teens and at least a minute by the time I was an adult. I loved watching her every single time she told this story. It was the only story of goodness she had of her childhood. All of the rest were bad, ironically producing no tears or faraway looks. She and Grandma Mary hemmed the coat and shortened the sleeves, being careful to leave all the material attached so as to let it out as she grew. When I would asked what happened to it, she would laugh and say, "My gosh, I wore it out!" I was ten before I realized Miss Parkins had taken off her own coat and wrapped Margaret in warmth that day—an act of kindness that my mom could never, would never forget. Until the Alzheimer's.

"How is your mom doing?" friends often ask. I never ever know what to say. It is my nature to always try and make people feel better. I used to believe this was my way of being liked, but I have learned it is genuine of me to actually want to be kind. So to answer this question with any amount of truth is next to impossible for me.

So I say, "The same." She is in this or that stage of Alzheimer's, but her appetite is good. She is happy, content. Some folks want me to elaborate, or there is a lull in the conversation mostly because they have no idea what to say next, so I sometimes throw in details like these: "She lights up when she gets ice cream." "She has never gone through that angry stage, so we feel blessed." This is not exactly the truth. I was with her as we withdrew her (cold turkey) from antidepressants. She was angry then, and she just missed my face with her clenched fist. Immediately she stopped herself and reached for me, saying that she was sorry, that she would never hurt me! She had no idea who I was, but like most visits she knew that I was someone she loved and someone who loved her.

Prior to my cold-turkey visit I had spent five days with her and thought those days would be my last time spent with her. I thought this almost every time that I saw her. I was reduced to uncontrollable sobs alone in my car after I left her on the fifth day. What was the trigger for the depth of my rage? She sat at a table with three other Alzheimer's patients eating their dinner. Some needed assistance; she did not at that time. This would change by my next visit. I had knelt down beside her and told her that I had to go. She said, "I wish you didn't." This like almost everything that she said surprised me. My family and I were not accustomed to her talking much, and when she did, it did not always make sense. Although at that time, it still sounded like English. This, too, would change by my next visit. I replied that I would be back. As I did, she reached for my face, cupping my cheek in her palm. I felt the softness of her hand, my eye caught the wrinkled spotted skin—her hand, with its long, boney fingers, nails painted red, a color applied by the staff that she had not worn on her nails since the forties, and I let the tears run down my cheeks. I reached up and gently placed my hand over top of hers as if I was moving in slow motion, and I let it rest there on my cheek. I moved toward her and leaned into kiss her cheek and told her that I loved her. As her dinner mates, my sister, a speech therapist, and a wife of another patient looked on we all were captured in a moment so much more powerful than any disease. This was a moment of pure love, and nothing could keep it away, not even Alzheimer's. By the time I reached my car, I could barely walk. I was shaken to the core with grief. In the safety of my car, locked in, sound-proofed and alone, the rage I felt at this disease poured out of me as if I were bleeding it.

I was a wanted child. I had always doubted this as I had come along long after it seemed to me my family was already complete—two parents and three kids neatly spaced four years apart. I came eight years after the fact. I asked my dad once if I was a mistake. He replied, "Hell, you all were." I found this hilarious and quite comforting. After the town clock had rang seven times, my brother Billy, who was eight years my senior, said he knew I was here. Apparently it was a long pregnancy for him, longer than for my mother, according to both. He wanted a little sister. He ran up the street to meet the approaching car bringing me home. I'm not sure how old I was when he began tormenting me, but he seemed nice until he began drinking. He was twelve years old. Tom, four years Billy's senior, drank too, but Tom by his own admission never found trouble like Billy did.

By the time I was two years old my dad had found he needed a bigger house, a bigger paycheck, and a bigger town—a town without so many nosy folks who knew everywhere he was at every moment of every day. He was working at the local auto parts store, and everyone needed auto parts. Everyone also seemed to need a drink, so if Bill wasn't at the auto store, he was at the local bar. This was not a town full of Mabels. There were only a few bars around the town square and a few scattered farther out of town, much too far of a drive for a man with a wife and four kids to get home to. So we moved to the big city Columbus, the capital, back when that meant something. For my dad it meant a new job—a better job with more money, more opportunity, and more clout. What it meant for my mom was no family, no friends, and too many Mabels. She would have to be brave.

My sister, Brenda, had begged to finish high school in Newark, so my family had stayed there while my dad drove back and forth between Columbus and Newark to his new job at Ohio Auto Parts. The trip took forty-five minutes each way, an enormous amount of travel time in a day before *freeways.* Brenda with her dark brown eyes and light auburn hair and, as she called them, her Elizabeth Taylor eyebrows was a popular high schooler. She had a steady boyfriend and lots of gal pals to hang out with. She had been crowned queen of some nonspecific dance and received good grades. What Margaret could not have foreseen when she decided to have another baby, was that when that child began to walk, her youngest son would be showing signs of emotional trouble; her oldest child would be stricken with rheumatic fever, bedridden for most of her senior year of high school, and all the while her husband would disappear 40 miles away for a better job in a bigger city.

Life was supposed to be getting easier. By a leap of faith thousands of parents had allowed a vaccine for polio to be administered on their children, and it had been a success. The war was over. The United States of America was feeling prideful and hopeful. My mother had discovered my cousin David's polio as he lay on the sofa and my sister read to him. Our house was put under quarantine; my sister was put under the spell of guilt for her own fear of catching the dreaded disease. David survived. My sister was spared from polio, and the quarantine was eventually (like all the other fear-filled homes touched by polio) lifted. My dad was no longer walking the neighborhood streets as a *watchman* leaving the house just before dusk, carrying a lantern, knocking on doors reminding folks to turn off their lights in order to avoid an attack from the enemy. However, Margaret never let life get easier. She had to stay vigilant; there was always a predator around every corner, just waiting to attack. Be it polio, war, a stranger with a dagger, or God forbid anything that made her cry, she could never let anyone see her cry.

Moving away from her mother, who wouldn't leave her own home during the long winter months for fear of the pipes freezing, was overwhelming for my mom. Grandma was the rock of the family. She made all decisions, good or bad, and her word was the final say. When my mother at the tender age of sixteen and my father being twenty-two went to Kentucky to marry, it was Grandma who calmed everyone down, saying, "He's a good man. I'll never have to worry about Margaret again with Bill taking care of her." It was the final word, and Mildred went along (as a witness) to Kentucky, a state where such marriages were legal. They had met when Margaret was thirteen years old outside the only evening entertainment in town for the local youth of Newark, Ohio, peeking in the windows of the Holy Rollers Church. Bill had courted Margaret for a long time and had flirted with Mary, telling her that he knew he would always have a beautiful wife when he married her daughter as she herself was so very beautiful. Although a bit shorter than all the sisters and their mother, he was handsome with a slight wave in his dark hair, kind, squinty eyes, devilish grin from a closed, thin-lipped smile that appeared to turn up only on one side and always dressed impeccably. Not to mention he was employed by the respectable Western Union Company and always appeared at the end of his day looking as though he had just started his day, even after delivery of many a telegram on his bicycle. By the time Bill purposed to Margaret, asking Mary for her daughter's hand, he had a new job and an automobile, a rare sight in 1935 in small town.

There is a picture of that car, a black-and-white, five-by-seven glossy with white trim on its edges, a picture of the car with its front end smashed and its windshield shattered, a hole in the passenger's side where Margaret's head hit and went through the glass. She came home from the hospital, looking like a mummy, her head completely wrapped in white bandages. Brenda was Bill and Margaret's only child at the time. She had waited all day with Mary for Daddy to bring Mommy home, but when he did, Brenda ran screaming from the site of her mom. Margaret had not cried, not until then. Margaret had not been angry. After all they had both had a few drinks, but she was the one who suggested maybe they stay over and not drive. It was late, very dark, and they were *tired*. That was then, before her own four-year-old ran screaming from her arrival. Bill had said he was fine; it wasn't far and not that late. She protested weakly. Who was she angry with? She wasn't sure, but she was angry and had nowhere to put that anger save the place she put all the other—away in her heart.

Mary stayed close during Margaret's recovery—the headaches, bandage changes, and Margaret's anguish over not being able to remember the accident. She took Brenda out for adventures, watching the taffy-pull machine set up in the window of the town's only candy store, spreading a blanket out to watch the local boys play baseball and to run errands to the post office, to get the newspaper, and to visit Kroger for groceries for each of the four weeks that past. Brenda, who was too young to remember much of this time, remembers only a handsome, blue-eyed man walking toward her grandmother and herself on one of these trips to Kroger. He was sharply dressed in what my dad would call, "his Sunday go-to meeting" clothes, and he carried a brand-new doll baby lightly clasp and daggling in his hand opposite the arm carrying a small brown paper sack clasped tightly at its top in the other. Brenda noticed the doll baby and the bag. She wondered if the bag contained baby-doll clothes. Mary grasped Brenda's hand tighter, something Brenda was used to from Mommy whenever a stranger approached. But this blue-eyed man was no stranger; there was something familiar about him and something kind. Grandma spoke to him first, only using his name, "Ed." She had stopped in front of him, holding Brenda's hand increasingly tighter. "Mary." That was all that was said between the two of them, their names, and as they spoke, Brenda's little hand was beginning to hurt. Ed looked down at Brenda and smiled. She could have sworn his eyes twinkled. Grandma was pulling her granddaughter around the man with the doll, and as she walked away from him and toward Kroger, Brenda walked sideways, looking back at the familiar stranger walking away from Kroger. And as she did, he turned and winked. "He could have given you that doll," was all Mary said as she loosened her grip on Brenda's little redden hand.

Mary and Ed were separated, had been for years. It was never a legal separation; it was just that when Ed went on a drinking binge, Mary would up and change their residence. Newark was small. It didn't take him long to find *his* home, but it took a while. It took until Christmas Eve the last time Mary was to ever *let him in*. Mary's hay fever had been worse than ever this particular year, and even as the last autumn leave had fallen, she was still suffering; however, with the arrival of the first snow she was feeling much better. By Christmas Eve the coldness in her heart for the man who provided she and her children with nothing but grief was lifting. As her bed grew colder and her loneliness intensified, she was feeling the spirit of generosity and forgiveness. Ed knocked on the door well past 10:00 p.m. The girls thought it was Santa. Dorothy opened the door after the signal words "let him in." He was drunk. His eyes were set deep in crystal blue pools of blood.

His clothes were long since rumpled and dirtied from Mary's last wash and iron. His thinning blond straight hair lay flattened and shiny under his crushed gray wool cap. He had no beard but only a dark shadow of an unshaven, dirt-streaked face. He stumbled in and almost immediately tripped over his own haphazard walk while he simultaneously yelled out, "Merry Christmas." Margaret, small enough to fit, ran behind the wood-burning stove and would not come out until Joe assured her it was their dad and not some nightmarish version of a horrid Santa. Joe told her to be brave and come out before she missed the real Santa. That worked. She was very brave, and everyone said so. The real Santa showed up every year without fail in a big truck with

the words "The Salvation Army" on the side. The real
Santa brought beautifully bright orange, glorious sweet-
smelling oranges from a far-off land in a basket neatly tied
with a Christmas bow.

Chapter Three

I was always sick on Christmas. The house would be decorated festively, the presents wrapped creatively, using holiday cards from previous years and saved paper wrappings, and I would be checked on for a cough, a sore throat, a fever, or some sort of spots—hives, chicken pox, measles, sumac, or "just a rash." Mom loved to decorate, and nothing would stop her Christmas, not even being a good mother. She would do both. Many years later after we had moved her into a *retirement* facility and taken away her car, the only access she had to buy anything was at the facility's little drugstore in the lobby. Tom had brought over a fresh Christmas tree for her, but because he, his wife, Donna, and I could not figure out where one of us kids had put the boxes of Christmas decorations, she had nothing to put on her Christmas tree. By the time my family and I arrived from California to spend Christmas with her, she had purchased about a dozen round, white, nylon-netted body scrubbers and hung them on her tree by their ropes. No one dared mention the apparent appearance of dementia these bath accessories were a sign of. When we were alone, she snuggled up to me and said, "What do you think of my snowballs on the tree?" I smiled and sighed a little too loud, to which she acknowledged, "I bet you all thought I was nuts putting those on there, but they do look like snowballs, don't you think?"

Had she been in her own home, those snowballs would have ended up in a bag in the basement, saved for another project or use down the road *someday*. She had lived through the Great Depression, and like most from that era, she had learned to save everything from bacon grease to paper milk caps from glass bottles, a little seemingly useless item that came to be a collector's item in the 1990s. I had cleaned out that basement when my mother's second husband had decided to move them into a retirement home. What we kids didn't know, what he never mentioned was that Mom had had *episodes*. She had been lost. Mom and Hal had met at a senior's dance. They were both widowers and had been for ten years each. Mom had grieved for my father. She had cried all the tears that she had held on to for so long. They came from every ounce of her being, and they came for two years. Dad died just before their fiftieth wedding anniversary.

My mother and I had sat by his bedside, taking turns holding his hand, and we watched him take his last breath. He had momentarily awoken the day before from a deep, morphine-induced sleep, and he had tried to speak. Tom was in the room at the time with Mother and me. He panicked. His love for our father told him to immediately call a nurse to pump in more morphine, thereby keeping him out of pain. I panicked too, but my love told me to let him speak regardless of the pain. I heard him. I had to lean in close. My tears spilt over onto his pillow, but I stayed close and let them fall, not daring to move or breath. With

23

what seem to be great effort he said, "I'm sorry. I love you all." The nurse had arrived. The morphine had been administered, and my mother had nearly collapsed.

She had been awake for nearly three days. The hospital had allowed us to bring in a comfortable chair for her to place beside his bed. She ate her meals there. She tried to read, and although she loved to read, she could not concentrate on the material, could not keep her dry, bloodshot eyes open long enough to finish a paragraph. I brought her herbal tea bags and talked her into placing one on each eye to allow the herbs to nourish her tired eyes, therefore manipulating her into some sleep. It was in this position—tea bags lying in the deep set sockets of her eyes with the strings and their paper tags dangling down both sides of her checks—that our minister found her sound asleep. I brought him in quietly, having asked him to see my father and to pray. She awoke with a start when we entered. She jumped just a little, but it was enough for the bags, which had lost all their moisture, to fall from her eyes and onto her breasts. My mom rarely laughed. When she did it was almost always at herself. She found this scene hysterical. It was the last time I would hear her laughter for many years.

Her second husband, Hal, was a good man; her mother would have thought so. He took care of Margaret while he lived, and he did so with his money after he died. Hal was hard of hearing, and he was Mormon—two things Margaret found frustrating. Soon after they were married, Hal wanted to be baptized for Bill, so he and my mom, according to his religion of choice (he was not born into Mormonism), would be together in the afterlife. Margaret found no need for this, but Hal found great need for it.

Margaret and Bill had a long life together, and they had children and grandchildren. Why would she not want to be with Bill and her family for all eternity? "I can do this for you and for Bill," he told her for months. Margaret was Lutheran. She, Bill, and all their children had been baptized. What was this new idea that made no sense? She tried to talk religion over with Hal; however, Hal was hard of hearing, and Margaret was stubborn about that. She was not going to repeat anything. Better to give in and just let him have his religious fantasy if it made him feel better. It did.

Hal first noticed there was something wrong when he dropped her off at the local mall *Northland*, making arrangements along the way for the time and location of his return to pick her up. It was a long, straight mall, no curves, turns, or second stories. She had stopped driving her own car after a small traffic accident that she was cited for. He knew his hearing was a problem, so he had made sure that they were on the same page. He waited for two hours at the agreed-upon location. She walked the mall, periodically sitting for those two hours, fuming that he was not picking her up. He went in to find her, and when he did, they argued. He expressed his concern for her; she expressed her anger at him. They settled nothing, and then she fell in the bathroom a month later. She was put into the hospital. What happened the day of the fall no one knew; however, she had had *episodes*, and this one took her down. Like the car accident that forced her head through a windshield decades before, she remembered nothing.

Margaret lived in denial. You won't find this in any of the scientific Alzheimer's information pamphlets, but what better way to bury pain than deny its existence?

Alzheimer's has to be, if there is one, the ultimate denial disease. Denial protects. It denies that you have lost two husbands, that a son has fallen into alcoholism, a source of pain for you beyond all others. It denies that your own beloved mother, suffering from dementia, told you that she hated you, as you stood by and watched strangers carry her off. Away to a place that you thought would be safe and she would be cared for, as you no longer could because you were worn down to your very core. It denies that her dying there within two days is your fault. You can *forget* that your father abandoned you time and time again in fields, barbershops, and your own home. Like her father before her with drink, Margaret's way out of pain was to forget.

She had tried to forget, but never would she forgive, not an event in her life that shook her to her soul. She was a teenager, working her first job at the local Newark five-and-dime store on the town square. She was working behind the cash register. She was so proud of herself for getting a job! She saw the man with the deep-set blue eyes enter long before he saw her. She had not seen those eyes in over a year. Mary had refused to move the children and herself to Baltimore, Maryland, for his promise of "a new barber job there in the fancy part of town." Mary had her study job at the cigar factory. It had never let her down, and Ed had. He had left, and no one knew that he was back. He was walking toward Margaret, and she was scared, excited, and apprehensive. Margaret had wanted to go to Baltimore. They had relatives there whom they had visited more than once, and she liked it there. She found the shops, the waterfront, and the row houses beautiful and orderly, the later appealing to her the most. She wanted to live in one of those houses. He was almost to her counter. He didn't look up into her eyes, only past her to the bottles and cans behind her in neat rows, stacked three to four deep on dark wooden shelves, seemingly made for each height of each product. His voice dichotomized into soft yet husky, his manner slow but seemingly urgent. "May I please have one of those bottles of the rubbing alcohol . . . please?" Only then did he look at her. Only then did she see the glaze over his eyes. Only then did she feel the hurt; hurt would turn to anger that she would have to swallow for the rest of her life. He did not know who she was, and she knew it. He did not recognize his own daughter, and worse yet he was asking her to sell him a cheap high. She sold him the bottle, and then she left her new job.

I asked her about this story many times after she had told it to me the first and only time. She would always say, "I don't remember any such story. I never had a job." The night that she had actually told me this story we had stayed up very late. I loved staying up late with my night-owl mother; it was the only time she would open up about her feelings and/or philosophical views on life. She believed in God and didn't understand anyone who did not. This may have come not from any church—certainly not the circus atmosphere around the outside windows of the Holy Rollers—but from her and her sibling's indoctrination to a Christian way of life during their summer camp adventures with The Salvation Army. We could never walk past a bell ringer for The Salvation Army at Christmastime without putting in a dollar or two and subsequently hearing how they had taken care of her as a child, and she didn't know how they all would have survived without The Salvation Army. I still don't walk by the bell ringers without putting in a dollar or two.

My father was agonistic when it came to matters of faith. He used to say that some men found God in a bottle, and what the hell was that? He knew Psalm 23 by heart though, so what the hell was that? Me, I prayed all day long and fell asleep only by praying. When I was sick, which was not just around Christmastime but every holiday and most of the winter school semester, I prayed to get better. When I was better, I prayed not to get sick. I prayed for every member of my family and all our relatives. I prayed for every neighbor on our street. I prayed for every animal I saw running lose. (Somehow, the ones in yards seemed safe. I no longer feel that is necessarily true.) And I prayed for every child in every country who had no supper. This did not include America because as kids we were never told that there were starving children in America. We were told to clean our plates because of the starving children in China, Africa, and Appalachia. (I thought this was another country.) To this adage my brothers would reply as brothers all over the country would reply, "Then let's send them the food."

This would infuriate my mother every time. So one day she hauled us off to Big Bear grocery store, where we packed to the top two grocery carts full of cans and boxes of food. The weekend consisted of filling up boxes of canned food and boxes of cake mix to send to starving children. I have no idea if they really went out of the country. My guess is they went to The Salvation Army, but my brothers didn't say that again for at least a month of Sundays! I prayed that the kids would like all the food, while I wondered how they were going to make cakes.

On rare occasions my parents would go out together without kids. On even rarer occasions my grandmother would be my babysitter. She was rarely in Columbus because of the pipes possibly freezing. (She would say this in July.) The best part about my grandmother babysitting was that she was hilarious. She would jut out her false teeth and then chase you around the house, yard, or bed. Nothing was more fun that this! I have no doubt that all her grandchildren would agree with me on this. The second best part was that we would bake. I always thanked God for the baking because I just knew that starving children did not get to bake with their grandmothers. You were allowed to lick the cake/frosting bowl, but under no circumstances were you allowed to eat the raw cookie dough as this would give you worms. My youngest cousin contracted worms, and my grandmother was convinced this was how it had happened. Of course at some point you just cannot *not* eat the raw cookie dough, so she would say that one or two bites probably wouldn't give us worms.

On one of these occasions my grandmother and I found a stray cat. It was a mess. Most likely it had worms. We gave it a drink of milk from the Frigidaire and made a box for it to sleep in. We presumed that a *lost cat* would want to be contained in a large box. Bad assumption. It was at first an adventure to be in a box, but after a while the cat went nuts, got out of box, and tore through my mother's orderly house. We had some explaining to do upon my parents' return . . . and fast. Grandma was convinced that I needed this cat. Her idea was to take the blame. "We played too much with the cat." She would keep the cat in bed with her, risking worms, thereby showing Mom the next day that it was a well-behaved critter. The next day Mom put the cat out. It stuck around the yard for as long as I kept sneaking it milk but was gone when I missed just one day. Grandma had gone back to Newark and had stayed with my younger cousin for her parents' night out. They didn't have an extra bed for Grandma. She slept with her charge, and years later we found out where my cousin's worms really came from. Apparently, according to Grandma, they came from the combination of a stray cat and raw cookie dough.

I have always loved animals. My mother always detested animals. You couldn't blame her really. Although not the youngest, being the smallest child in her family, it was logical that she be the one lowered into the outhouse to retrieve a fallen puppy. Ed had a brought home a peace offering to his family after he had been thrown in jail for what amounted to public drunkenness—public because he was in the street gutter, passed out, frightening children on their morning walk to school, one of which was Margaret with her sisters. Margaret loved the new puppy so much so that she took it everywhere with her, including the john in the middle of the night of its first night with its new family. Heavy-eyed, she had gone back to bed, wrongly believing the puppy was following her. The puppy's wails had gone unnoticed from the deep walls of the outdoor john until the morning's first visitor, Ed. Ed informed the family, and after he volunteered for the task at hand, it became clear that he wouldn't be able to accomplish retrieving the gift puppy from its smelly prison. Margaret was lowered in to perch on the inside crap-laden ledge above the real mess, where the puppy had had the luck to fall and spend its evening.

My mother never touched a dog or any other animal from that point on—save once. She always made us wash our hands at every restroom we past while we visited the Columbus Zoo, which I will admit was a pretty dirty place before Jack Hanna took it on. Billy, a future contributing sponsor/member of Jack Hanna's zoo, was the spoiled child. He had had a hernia as a tiny kid and you had to deal with him with kid gloves. This was carried into his adulthood and was a source of great contention from me. Like a cat trying to impress its owner, he brought home everything living and dead to present to my mother. She simply could not say no to him in regard to anything . . . ever. As a young family Bill and Margaret Larason had spent lots of family time at Buckeye Lake. Bill's sister, Pauline, had a cabin on the lake there along with a dock that kept a beautiful Kris craft boat and a couple of rowboats. The family often slept over here, drinking, playing cards, boating, and often attending the local amusement park.

Billy, a friendly and unruly kid, had wandered off on one of these day trips to the park. Margaret was out of her mind with worry and fear. He was eventually found sitting on the lap of the man in a folding metal chair, a man who took tickets at the fenced gate after they had been purchased at the entrance tower. My mother did not wait for an explanation from this man, who was explaining to my dad that he thought it best to keep the boy here with him as sooner or later his folks would have to leave the park in order to find him. She simply snatched little Billy up out of the man's lap while she yelled at him of his perversions. Bill was left to halt the ensuing panic at the entrance tower after he had heard the man's story and believed him. Margaret never forgot that she had almost lost her littlest boy to a pervert/kidnapper.

Billy was almost lost many times. My parents rarely knew where he was during his teen years. Attendance calls from the schools came monthly. Calls in the middle of night from police/hospitals came later. He made the papers, complete with a picture in the *Columbus Dispatch* after he crashed his car into a tree and the authorities freed him with the Jaws of Life. He married at nineteen years of age as did all Margaret and Bill's kids—all except me. He and his new bride moved to an adorable little beachfront house at Lake Erie. There they fought like cats and dogs, and his drinking sped out of control as did his driving. His wife had already witnessed one of his car crashes in front of her very eyes one night in Columbus as she had followed him home "so he would be safe." Her call from a Sandusky hospital on a cold November night came late when all terrifying calls seem to come. Billy was in the hospital with head trauma, and they didn't know if he would make it or not. He was unconscious when Margaret first saw him, his head torn apart from back to front. Margaret ended up renting an apartment in Sandusky while she and his wife waited for him to wake up. We had Thanksgiving dinner that year at White Castle, and by Christmas I was sick.

Chapter Four

I t was Valentine's Day 2007. My husband, Mark stood in our doorway with red roses, a red heart-shaped box of candy, and news of my brother Bill's untimely, unexpected, and strange death almost forty years after he had woken up from his coma in Sandusky, Ohio. Bill and I had spoken on the phone five times three days prior.

It was the most I had spoken to him on the phone in many years. I had written him out of my life to save my sanity. He had become a drunk—his words. To me he had become a weight that I didn't need. I had tried to save him. I sent him via US mail every piece of information on alcoholism—what it was, how to kick it, what it would do to one's health, family, and mind. His wife told me that he read everything, I didn't believe her. He thanked me for caring but said, "I'm a drunk, not an alcoholic."

I went to Al-Anon meetings. I sent his wife information about meetings in her area. It was at the meetings that I learned I had no power. That was news to me. I had always felt I had power over Bill. When I was young and my brothers would tease me physically or mentally, I learned to control my temper, my giggles, my physical reactions, whatever it took to make them stop. When I got older, I could beg for Bill's car keys and make him stay put when he was too drunk to drive. When all else failed, I could cry. It never went that far with Tom. He always stopped the kidding before I was too upset, but Bill would push on through with delight.

It was that delight that confused. I'd see it in his eyes. I'd feel it in his movements. I would have to figure out my modus operandi to make him stop. I learned the crying one night in our basement. My mom always said that a television set ruined any decorating scheme, so the TV had been relegated to the basement. Every Friday night without fail regardless of my self-confessed fear of both the basement and the Friday night late show called *Chiller Theater*, I would venture down the stairs to the "TV room." Mom thought it sounded better when we referred to the different parts of our basement as if they were actual rooms in a larger home: The TV room, the laundry room, the tool room. In the basement TV room I sat with my back to the stairs right smack in the middle of the sofa, legs crossed, ice cream bowl in hand, TV tuned to my show and ready to be scared out of my wits.

It was *The Phantom of the Opera*, the scene where there is a mirror, which was never a good sign, when Bill, who was as quiet as a mouse, grabbed with full force the front of my face, cupping his hand over my mouth and nose, and pulled my head back against the back of the sofa. I was kicking. I spilled my ice cream, my arms alongside of my hips, my thighs, trying to push myself up. Interestingly enough I never tried to remove his hand from my face. I thought he was killing me, and I could hear him laughing. I wanted to go limp. That worked for tickling, but I was fighting for my life, not my ticklish foot. I started to cry, not real tears but the movements that one's body makes when one cries—the shoulders up and down, the back in and out—and then I went limp.

He let go. But I never did. I never watched *Chiller Theater* again (which was probably not a bad thing). I avoided the basement until my dad, always up on the latest new toy, brought home a round rope swing (now outlawed in every state). Given that it was winter, he hung it from the rafters in the basement. Billy and I spent hours on that swing. He got the clever idea to position the sofa so that you could stand on the arm, and then someone could push you off at an alarming speed, twirling round and round uncontrollably, your legs tightly entwined with each other, your crotch seemingly clutching the rope in the middle of the swing, and your hands and arms holding the top of rope above your head. Two weeks into the popular swing, I stood almost ready on the arm of the sofa, my bottom planted squarely on the swing seat. Billy pushed me before I was fully ready. In other words I wasn't holding on yet. I was adjusting my shorts so that I would not get a rope burn.

I flew. When I woke up flat on my back, my head throbbing, my parents were kneeling next to me, telling me to catch my breath, and Billy was crying. He was also yelling, "I killed her. I killed her." I could hear him like he held a megaphone in my ear. Everything else sounded far away. My parents' voices, the music we had had playing, all sounded like it was in a cave, but Billy was loud and clear. All I could think was this: *He really does love me*, and I was going to milk that for all it was worth. I stayed still, and when my breath came back, I tried to hold it. I wanted to turn blue. My dad caught on and said that they would have to take me to the hospital. My brother's sobs got louder. I began to breath. I had power over Billy.

Did it start then? Is that when I learned that if I didn't breath I would get attention? I had had small panic attacks before as a very small child. The first was when I was baptized. Being the last child, getting through the move to the city, getting through her oldest child's illness, I guess Mom had a rough time fitting in a baby getting baptized, so I was old enough to walk to the baptismal fount. I walked from my seat in the back of Saint Paul's Lutheran Church in Newark, a church that I had no memory of but one that had been my parents' church, and all other children of Margaret and Bill's had been baptized here as babies. My whole extended family was there, or so it seemed. I saw my aunts' smiling faces as I began my journey up toward the front of the church. As I passed each row, another smiling relative would be gazing lovingly at me, and with each one I could feel my hands getting slimier, my heart racing faster, and my vision growing narrower. I have no memory of the actual procedure as it were, but I have a certificate of baptism, so I assumed it went down as planned.

The next aisle to walk was as flower girl in my sister's wedding. I was four years old, adorable with wisps of blond hair and wearing a knee-length pink crepe dress that was fit for a princess with white ankle socks laced at their edges, wearing patent leather white shoes. We had rehearsed my walk as well as the whole ordeal the night before. I was excited and proud to be doing the whole walk thing the next day, complete with a basket of real flower petals that I was to lie down before my beautiful sister's feet hit each step on her way to her prince. One problem was that I didn't know that the prior night's empty pews would be full of folks for the major event. I thought—and I remember this clearly—that if we rehearsed it then that meant everything would be the same, except we would all look beautiful for the wedding. On the day of the wedding as we the wedding party stood in the foyer and the doors were opened to reveal a full church, a long aisle covered in a white sheet, the prince in full US Air Force formal attire at the altar, and everyone looking at me, I went limp. My mother saw this and grabbed my little body to steady me. She tried to coax me. Then she tried to reassure me. Then she begged me. Then she walked me down the aisle. I don't remember anything else, but I know I wanted to throw those real rose petals out of my basket. But I couldn't move anything other than my feet.

It's been that way my whole life. Like with the rose petals, I always want to take the action, but it's all I can do just to get through, I never get to metaphorically throw the rose petals. If you have anxiety issues, I know you know what I mean here. Kindergarten was my next panic situation. I was excited to go. Margaret, Bill, Brenda, Tom, and Billy had all been telling all the wonders of it. It sounded like an absolutely amazing wonderland of a place. My mom had no car at the time, so we had a long walk to the school, the longest walk I had ever been on, but my feet were like little skipping stones, feeling all the excitement that anticipation has to offer an almost-six-year-old. We arrived with a lot of others, and there was a lot of talking and meeting, shaking hands, smiles, laughter, bending down for kisses and hellos and good-byes. I saw rooms with walls that didn't meet the ceiling, one with miniature furniture, a stove, a Frigidaire, even a red-brick cardboard fireplace. There was a room seemingly made out of blocks of a million colors. Turtles and fish, and was that a snake? There were shelves of books and boxes of crayons, chalks, and paints. My eyes were wide. I could actually feel them stuck open. Then it happened. My mother was the one bending down to me. She was kissing me and saying good-bye and telling me to have fun. Mrs. Gump, a gentle, soft-smiling soul was taking my hand and leading me away from my mother. This wasn't happening. No one had told me that Mom wasn't staying. Mom never left me anywhere!

She left me there to fend for myself with no instructions on how to do that. My hands were drenched the whole day. I felt the weight of my heart in my little chest as we laid our heads down on the table that we had cleared moments before of crayons and paper for nap time—a time I would look forward to for the rest of the long school year. This was a time when I could suck my thumb and pray to live through this colorful, strange, active, and independent place away from the safety of my mom. That first day a bell rang, which I learned meant recess. All of the other children ran like released prisoners out to the playground. I sat on the steps by the door so that when the bell rang for us to line up and come back in, I would not miss it or heaven forbid get locked out. There was no bell. Mrs. Gump came up to the stairs, put her hand on my shoulder, and blew a whistle. She smiled down at me and said, "Maybe tomorrow you would like to join the other children." She was so kind. She didn't force or push or belittle. She just suggested. So for all of kindergarten

I hung out by Mrs. Gump's side and God bless her—she let me.

Many years later I learned that it was she who had told my parents that I still sucked my thumb and that she believed this behavior was a sign of anxiety. My mom put something horrible-tasting on my thumb every morning before school. I sucked right through it, and she gave up. It had been all she could do to wrangle away my blanket before that year. I did enjoy kindergarten though. I usually stayed in the coatroom during the cold months for as long as I could to deal with my nerves. We would arrive, and depending on the weather, we would take off multiple layers. I loved winter because that meant more layers complete with boots, which meant longer stays alone in there. There was a boy who liked me and me him. Apparently he was aware of my coatroom hideaway because he sneaked in and kissed me. Hence, I liked kindergarten.

My years of elementary school became my sanctuary. Home was becoming a contentious place. My sister was gone and had a family of her own. My brother Tom had been drafted, and Grandma had us convinced he would be sent to Vietnam. Billy was in trouble at school, home, or the neighborhood constantly. Dad worked late, came home smelling of beer, and then retired with a beer to the basement to work more. My mom yelled at everyone all the time. I stayed in my room and played with my imaginary family. At first I was always the mother with several children, all girls and one boy, since Raggedy Andy was the only boy doll that I had. We had an idyllic life together. Later it was Barbie dolls, and I was always a victim of some sort of abuse from Ken. He would love me and then rape or hit me or vice versa. I blame this on the "sex in cinema" segment of my brothers' *Playboy* magazines. Seeing *Who's Afraid of Virginia Wolf* didn't help much either because I was afraid of her. Various other movies confused and fascinated me. There was no rating system, and nothing was off limits to me on television or the movie houses. There seemed to be a lot of anger in the world that I didn't understand.

Billy got his driver's license, and anger turned to fear. There were several late-night calls and trips to jails and hospitals and car lots where wreck cars are towed. My mother was coming unglued. She always put on her brave face and her high heels, walking into each situation with perfect posture. In those days a woman's worst fear was that she be caught by someone she knew with her hair in curlers or worse yet pin curlers. She used to say that she would just die if she had to go to a hospital in pin curls. My grandma still used rags to roll her hair and sleep on it at night and didn't understand why everyone didn't do this—problem solved. The bigger problem and the bigger fear was money. Billy was costing a fortune.

No one in my family believes the following story, but I was there. Mom and I used to dress up and take the bus downtown. We would go to the Lazarus department store and head straight to the candy counter, a four-sided glass heaven of chocolate delights. (Not even See's makes a counter like this was anymore.) And we would buy at least a dozen chocolate turtle candies. One we would each eat on site, and another on the bus on the way home. The rest I never saw again. Neither did anyone in the family. We would shop for her and shop for me. I could never get all that I wanted. This place was no Woolworths. It had an amazing plethora of styles, colors, and true to its name departments. We would cross an ally after we had seen all of Lazarus and go to a little privately owned dress shop. Here they served tea and had a candy dish out on a coffee table surrounded by four upholstered chairs with burgundy fabric. This isn't the part no one believes.

Mom and I set out on this journey once—only the bus kept going, or rather we stayed on the bus. At any rate we ended up in Newark. We got off in an unfamiliar part of town. Even though I didn't live there and hadn't grown up there, I knew it well from trip after trip there. We walked quite a ways, she in heels and a veiled hat, carrying a black patent leather purse with a gold clasp and single strap. She switched between clutching it to her chest and letting hang loosely from her hand. In her other hand she held mine as I tried to keep in step with her stride, in a dark blue plaid dress with a delicate white collar, my favorite black patent leathers, and bobby socks. We walked across the railroad tracks. I knew I had never been here before. There were row houses. I had never seen row houses before, but I understood their name now. They were not particularly charming in any way but curious in every way. First of all we were "on the wrong side of the tracks," and my mother was hurting my hand with her grip. As we approached the houses my mother bent down to me and said, "Be on your best behavior."

Given what I am about to tell you, this was ironic since the only other time we kids were told to be on our best behavior was when we went to Aunt Virginia and Uncle Forest's for Thanksgiving dinner in their big fancy house on the right side of the tracks. Mom knocked on the door of the house smack dab in the middle of the row.

There was a clay flowerpot with a red rosebush in full bloom on the stoop, the only life I had seen save weeds since we crossed the tracks. A woman yelled that she was coming and to hold our horses. The woman opened the door slightly as she gathered her floor-length, rose-embossed robe close to her body. As she adjusted her eyes to the light, she began tying the black silk robe and said, "Oh, my gosh, Margaret dear, come right in."

She opened the door wide for us and patted my head and said, "Aren't you just a sight?" I had no idea what kind of sight I was, but I had just entered quite a sight. All I could see in front of me was what appeared to be one room, a bed to my right with a mostly pink-flowered, cotton curtain tied loosely back with thick red rope that could be pulled all the way around the bed when loosened. The woman in the silk robe quickly did just that as we entered this room. A very small kitchen lay in front of me. There was a small fridge and a stove anyway. The tea kettle was whistling, and the woman, whom I had decided was beautiful, with disheveled blonde hair and blue eyes hidden by dark black eye makeup, was telling us we were just in time for tea. There was a room to the left partly shielded by yet another flowered curtain, this one favoring mostly greens, hanging from a rod over the doorway, visible because of a small blue light coming from its interior. My mother was telling *Aunt Dory* that she was sorry, that she should have called. "Well, I just didn't think that during the day there . . . well, that there would be a guest."

I didn't see another guest, but then the curtain around the bed opened slightly, revealing yet another pink rose pattern—a spread of chenille rather than the cottons and silks I had quickly grown accustomed too. Wrapped in the pink chenille lay a gorgeous man of (I'm guessing) Italian decent with slicked-back jet-black hair in a Marlon Brando *Streetcar Named Desire* T-shirt. He spoke. I have no idea what he said because the woman, to whom I had yet to be introduced but whom I had learned was named Dory, rushed over, ripped the curtain from his hand, and told him to go back to sleep until she told him otherwise. Impressive. Mother asked to speak to Dory privately, so I was sent to the stoop with the roses in clay pots.

Mother and Dory went behind curtain number two, the room with the blue light. The front door was left open, and I had a bowl full of Dory's candy in my lap. Their meeting was quick, and I heard the snap of Margaret's purse's golden clasp. They both came out to the stoop, and Mom began thanking and hugging Dory. Margaret reached for my hand, and I stood while I gazed from one woman to another in wonder. I left with another pat on the head and a white-lace ladies' hankie full of candy and much to my delight a gold, scalloped lipstick case containing a red lipstick. Mom confiscated the lipstick later, but I got to keep the gold case. She had taken the lipstick out and placed it in her handbag; the case she put in my hand and folded my little fingers around it. As she did she asked me not to tell my father about this adventure. I didn't. And until she had Alzheimer's I never mentioned it to anyone. When I told Tom, he flat out called me crazy. Brenda said she knew of no one like that. Dory was my grandfather's sister, and she was a hooker, although some say she was a *madam*. My aunt Mildred confirmed my story, but not until I was fifty years old! Dory also left Mildred money to take care of Ed when she died. I don't know anything other than what I've said here about Aunt Dory, but I can tell you this: She was beautiful and generous. Oh, and I have always wanted flowered curtains, a silk robe, and flowers on my stoop.

Chapter Five

I had to be a grown-up. I was helping my now-orphaned, forty-year-old niece, Charlotte, plan a double funeral. I would have to dip into the basket and pull out the petals, talk to literal flower people for the floral arrangements, which I botched badly because of nerves, and meet with funeral directors. I was a nervous, emotional wreck. Mom was my sanctuary now. Alone with her in the Alzheimer's unit I could think, grieve, and plan. It was during one of these visits with Mom that my daughter called hysterically crying and told me that her cat had died, and she said, "By the way, I'm married, and my husband has testicular cancer."

I was stunned. I had seen her name come up on the phone and had one of those mother moments when you know that it's your child just before it rings. I braced myself, always glad to hear from her but knowing it often meant trouble. She was crying. It took her a while to get the words out that her cat, *Jenifur*, who had slept on her pillow every night since she was three years old, was gone; however, her anguish was deep and there was fear.

She had graduated from high school and moved out to room with a girlfriend and attend Long Beach State. That had not lasted long. She hated college and said, "It's just like high school, only everyone smokes." Couldn't blame her really; she had gone to an arts school for three years. Each day's classes went from morning until 5:00 p.m., and then if she was in a show, musical theater being her major, she could be at school until 9:00 or 10:00 p.m. She had no life other than school and had taken college classes already. She was burnt out. She left the arts school and graduated from her neighborhood high school. It was a good decision for her, but her dad and I fought her on it. It wasn't easy to get into the arts school, and we were proud.

Her years at the arts school had been tumultuous. There was a lot of pressure academically and for productions. The drama wasn't just on the stages. There was constant rejection from constant auditions. She had had a regretful breakup with a boyfriend. She was very thin, and there were rumors of anorexia (although she said the good thing about actors is they say it to your face since they save the acting for stage). Her skin was showing signs of extreme adolescent stress. She was tired all the time, and her dad continued to push her to do more. Mark was a musician, a one-time musical theater guy, and he wanted for his daughter what he never had for himself. Typical.

She was breaking down. Then she met a boy who was tall, blond, and gorgeous, and he fell for her. And her damaged ego and wrecked body needed the boost. I knew he was trouble the first time I meet him. He would build her *up an*d then begin to tear her down. Because of my own depression issues and those in my family, I could see that she was showing signs of depression, and in that altered state of mind, she was not making wise choices. I hurried her off to a shrink or two. I hurried her off to a shrink or two. Needless to say, I was a wreck and worried out of my mind. Mark was not getting it. He didn't think his daughter could do any wrong, or any wrong be done to her especially by her own hand.

She was perfect. I was overreacting. She made sure that I was getting it. She told me as much as she could manage to speak of, and what she didn't tell me she left for me to find written, overheard, or acted out. She got through both high schools, alive, not pregnant, disease—and drug-free, but not unscathed. She had gone through depression and teenage angst, and since I had never given her tools to deal with what life throws one's way, she had no one to help her. I had made sure since she was a small child that she could get out of every mess on her own, believing foolishly that when it came down to you, you can only rely on yourself. What she learned was to not ask for help.

Here's the best example: She had had swimming lessons at the YMCA's "Diaper Dipper" and graduated with flying colors, so two weeks later when she slipped off a step where she had been sitting and playing with a friend in a pool, leading into three feet of water, I stood by the side and encouraged her, "Make it to the edge, baby. You can do it." All she was depending on was for her mom or Dad to reach in and save her, but I made her do it herself, with folks at the pool watching me, as if I was Joan Crawford (also known as Mommy Dearest). There are many more examples of this kind of self-saving that I gave her, but you get the idea. She was terrified, but she did it. I go over this kind of thinking time and time again. When she called me that day, hysterical over a loss, a cancer, and an impending responsibility, beyond anything that she had given any thought to, from three thousand miles away, having made a decision on her own in an act of both love and rebellion, I knew she was going to have to grow up fast.

I couldn't move as I continued to listen to her story, just barely getting out, "Why did you get married?" I'm sure that stunned her. From all she just told me, this was what I asked? I was feeling faint. Sandy, who ran the unit where my mom was and who was aware of our whole family's situation, saw me and moved in to push a chair under me as I went down heavy, cell in hand, holding my breath, emotions, and disbelief inside me. After my daughter and I hung up our phones, Sandy stayed with me and listened to my story. She was in charge of a room full of old folks who look affected by some sort of figment of Stephan King's imagination, yet she sat with me until I could breath. I told her, "I have to call my husband, and I don't know how I'm gonna break this to him." I needed him to go to her. She was in Portland, Oregon, where she had met up with her "just a friend" and married him.

After she dropped out of college, Mark had a fit that didn't stop for a long time. She finished her yearlong commitment to her roommate and lease and then moved back home for a short time before she took off in the middle of the night for Oakland, California. I begged her to allow me to drive with her, get her set up and fly myself home, but to no avail. She said she needed to do this on her own. Mark helped her pack her car, while I cried in my bed, both because of her unknown future and because I couldn't call my mother to have her listen to my woes. We had taken the phone out of her life, as not only did she no longer understand it's usage, she actually found the ring disagreeable. She would come home for Christmas. She called me from the road and said, "I can't do this. I can't face Dad, and I can't talk to him." I told her then turn around and go back. She came. Her "good friend" Shawn came over Christmas night. We all enjoyed each other's company. Mark said that "they're more than friends."

It doesn't happen often, but when Mark is right, he is right. They fell in love after a long friendship on a camping trip in Big Sur, California, and he said he was going marry her someday. Marry her he did without asking her old-fashioned dad for her hand. Mark had a fit again. It began with my phone call to tell him that she was married as well as the cancer part. I needed Mark to go to them. They were apparently living in a car and staying with assorted "friends" and couch-surfing. She had left her job and apartment in Oakland with the promise of an awaiting apartment in Portland. Seems everyone in Portland was waiting for an apartment.

Mark went to Portland. Once there, because of the cancer, he found himself biting his tongue; there was no apartment, no job, no money, nor any prospects from our son-in-law. As it was to turn out in the years to follow, Lacey became Shawn's meal ticket; although grateful for Lacey seeing him through his illness and recovery, he wouldn't pull himself away from chronic drinking, video gaming, joblessness and verbally abusive language towards her. Several years into their marriage, as she ran from yet another one of his temper tantrums, into their bedroom, locking the door behind her, he put his fist clean through the door, she left. She called me later to ask me to be with her (waiting outside) as she collected her dog, a few belongings and told her husband she was leaving him, "I'm not going to wait for him to hit me." I sat in the parking lot of their building, waiting as we sent text back and forth, both of her packing progress and conversation with Shawn; he's sober; he's ok; he's calm; almost done; all's well; you can go; I didn't leave, but I was losing daylight and began to feel panic, as I was losing visibility of their staircase. Then I saw her start to descend the stairs, with her little dog, Linus in step behind her, she was carrying her childhood teddy bear and a small bag of belongings. Seeing my daughter start down those stairs and walk away that day, so young, so hurt and so strong, was extremely sad; yet I was so filled with pride at that visual, that I could do nothing but stare at her and sob. Turns out brave runs in the family.

I stayed in Columbus and continued to make funeral arrangements. Billy's wife had gone by ambulance to the hospital on a cold winter day in 2007. She had long-suffered with COPD. She had filled out all the proper documentation to die naturally after the Terri Schiavo fiasco that had been all over the news media, even prompting former president Bush to get involved in her life verses death drama. Bill talked her into a trip together to the hospital and a breathing tube to save her life. It seemed better than taking her last labored breath in their hallway. He then went home and called Tom, asking him to come over and keep him company. They had not been on the best of terms since my dad had died in 1980. It was nothing specific, just old sibling rivalry stuff that seemed to always rear its ugly head after the death of a parent. The kind of unresolved issues that you didn't even know existed and different lifestyles had kept them apart. Tom and his wife went and spent the evening. Bill and I had spoken several times that day, and I had asked him to call me back with an update on her condition. When Tom left, Bill said, "I can't forget to call Christie." He didn't. He called four times. During each one he sounded worse. During one of the calls he said, "I cannot live without that woman. I love her more than my last breath." The last thing that I said to him was to just close his eyes and rest.

My niece called Tom, concerned about the fact that the hospital said Bill had not been there. It had been days. Tom told her he would drive over to the house to check on him. Columbus was having one hell of an ice storm. There was no one out but the snowplow drivers. He pulled up to a house that had all the signs of being unkempt for a few days, newspapers piled up, snow left un-shoveled, outside lights burning in the light of day—all things Bill would never do. He was immaculate about his yard, even when it was covered in snow. He knocked and checked doors and windows. There was nothing, no response. The car could be in the garage. He called the police, who called the fire department, who broke into the house and then asked Tom to identify the body lying over the bathtub.

He had had a heart attack. They said there was no reason to investigate further. All signs suggested that, but did he want them to go further? It could be something else. Tom said no. They said, "That's best." Their daughter had to decide if she wanted to have her dying mother brought out from under heavy sedation to tell her that her husband was dead. The breathing tube was also due to come out before it adhered to her skin. She was told and she had no response other than a few tears rolling down the darkened, hollowed-out cheeks of her face, cheeks attached to a head that looked as though it was being swallowed up by her pillow. I arrived in time to brush her hair, rub her feet, and watch her waste away, looking like a living, barely breathing skeleton without a voice above a whisper that she only spoke in between coughing fits, so weak that each one seemed her last.

We all waited for her to die with Bill on ice. We couldn't wait much longer because he couldn't, so he was cremated, and we waited some more. She died, and we did not know if she knew. She never mentioned him. I believe that she just did not have the strength to grieve and die, so she chose dying. Tom called the funeral director, whom he had called for Billy during an ice storm on a cold February day in 2007 and for my dad in 1980, and then he and his wife left on a planned vacation with all of our blessings. He had been through enough. Charlotte began her ordeal with the hospital and the estate. I called the flower people and told them I needed an arrangement for a coffin and an arrangement for in front of an urn, both of which Charlotte and I had picked out together, as five of her kids sat in comfortable funeral parlor chairs. I failed to tell the florist that it was for two people. Hence, we had a long conversation during which neither of us understood why the other didn't comprehend. "Mrs. Wood, you should just need one arrangement. That is all most people do. Then usually other people send flowers, and those can be arranged nicely around the urn or the coffin."

"Listen, funeral professional, flower person. Why don't you understand what I want? I want something for both!" We went around and around until it finally dawned on me, and I explained the double funeral thing to a woman I felt should have figured this out on her own. I still think that. They only did funerals!

It served its purpose for me though. I knew I had to calm down. I had to calm down enough to face yet another bunch of rose petals and throw them out in all directions. Lacey had come to Ohio to be with us and to attend the service. She spent time with her grandma, attending to her hair, makeup, and fingernails, always making her grandma laugh just as she had always done. With all Lacey had gone through in her young life, she always made sure to make Grandma happy. No one wanted to speak at the funeral. Shirley's brother was making a lot of arrangements for how the service was to go down, and one of them was for someone to speak for each of the deceased. He would speak for Shirley. As her brother, his wife, my brother, his wife, my husband, my sister, and my daughter sat in Tom's family room, sipping on our various alcoholic drinks, Shirley's brother looked to Tom to speak for Bill. Tom said, "I can't." It was actually quite a sight. Tom was always my go-to-in-a-crisis guy. He was everyone's go-to guy in a crisis. He was my rock. He was the first guy to ever hold my hair when I threw up. Everyone knows that's the go-to guy. He had first held my hair after I heard funny noises against the aluminum trash can lid when I was taking out the trash. That was never my chore, but I seemed to always be doing it. The noise was frog legs still jumping, but they were not attached to any frogs. I screamed and cried, and then with my mom and Tom looking on, I threw up. He dove toward me for the hair rescue. The irony is that he and Billy had been frogging.

The next time he dove in to save my hair was in the parking lot of the hospital where we were leaving our brother, who was in a coma. The next happened at another hospital where my father would die. He was my rock, and he was not going to save me this time. He was too devastated. I owed him. I owed everyone. I owed Billy for disowning him. I would speak. I loved him. I didn't love that he drank, much less that when he drank he was violent; however, I would find the good, for there was a lot of good, and I would make him make sense to me.

It was after Shirley had attended one of the area's Al-Anon meetings that she told me Billy sometimes hit her.

She said, "It's only when he's been drinking." Problem with that was that he was always drinking. I told her to leave him. She never did. He left her. And then our family buried them both. What a love story. It started during Billy's first marriage. Bill and Donna, Tom and Donna, both boys married Donnas. Bill and Donna were high school sweethearts, and they married at nineteen, just like Tom, just like Brenda. I was old at twenty-three! Margaret *loved* Donna or "Little D," as we called her. I always thought this was because she married after Tom and "Big D" married. Later someone told me it had to do with their sizes. Margaret loved both her daughter-in-laws, but there was a mothering going on with Little D, a taking-in if you will. It was odd, considering that Tom's wife had been literally taken in to live with us when he went to basic training for the US Army. But Big D had a way of taking charge that little D did not. When she moved in, I had just gotten the whole upstairs to myself, so I was darn resentful that I was relegated to a small corner without a door for privacy while she got the main room—something she had no way to understand coming from a family of eight kids in a small farmhouse. I had always enjoyed my privacy and as a teen girl really loved getting the boys old roomy private space. I became quite the whinny brat. Margaret's generosity with her home, as well as her sense of family, gave her much grief from me. But that was the least of her problems.

Shirley was the *other woman*, and she stayed that way for much of her and Bill's marriage. Margaret was none too happy that Little D was out, that Shirley was in, and that my mom's perfect family had been tarnished and dismantled. Mom and Dad lost Brenda's husband from a perfect family scenario as well. He and my sister divorced after nineteen years of marriage under very fishy circumstances. Suffice it to say that Brenda lost a husband and a best friend who had lived next door. Big D and Margaret became very close and stayed that way until my dad died. That was when everyone fell apart. Dad was a man of little words, but when he had them, he had you. Whether he was saying something funny or poignant or reiterating his overused mantra of "let's not to mention this to your mother," you listened when he spoke. Whereas Mother could go for days about this or that issue and you could keep the fight up with her, breaking her down as you went, Dad said something only once, and that was the final word. He died like that—no medication other than that for pain, no surgeries other than those to find the problem, no treatment by chemo or radiation, just having his final word. Margaret, on the other hand, was breaking down and apart, her brain turning to oatmeal, yet she was still bravely not going down without the fight.

"Thank God she doesn't know that her favorite son is dead." This is what we all said, and those of us who didn't were thinking it. It wasn't that she would be any less swallowed up by grief if it was one of her other kids, but Billy would have just broken her in a way that the rest wouldn't have. She would have put on her high heels for the rest of us and stood up with perfect posture for the survivors, but Billy was her unhealed heart, her project, her unfinished business. He was food for her denial. He wasn't a drunk. She said, "He only drinks beer." He and Donna didn't break up their marriage. Shirley did. "He didn't hit that tree. The police even said there was no way to tell which boy was even driving." "He didn't hit that tree. The roads were slick." "The snow was blinding. There was no way he could see the road, much less that pole." "We don't even have that kind of soap. They're crazy to think Billy soaped their windows." It went on and on.

When I spoke at his funeral, one of the stories that I told without much of the following detail or commentary was endearing to me. It was Christmas Eve, and we were going to the midnight church service. Billy said he would be there, but please could he attend with his friends? We spent most of the time at the service looking for Billy. He arrived home later that night for his drilling. After I had waited up for him with heavy eyelids and a safety pin to pick at the skin of my fingers until they bled—a practice designed not so much to keep me awake but one that I had found lessened my nerves—I planted myself behind the big blue high-back chair in the living room, the same chair I was interrogated in from time to time. Billy was told to sit in the chair, and then he was asked first by Dad and then by Mom, "How many trees are on the altar?" He answered Dad, but since he had given the wrong answer, Margaret was just sure that he had made a mistake and that given more time and thought he would be able to say the correct answer. I was behind the chair, giving him the correct answer. I could save this whole mess! He didn't believe me and continued down his path of ruin. He was grounded. That never meant anything.

He always believed me from then on, and when I told him during his first phone call in February of 2007 that Shirley would be okay, he said, "You always say the right thing." I don't know if that was the right thing, but I do know that I did right by the dead at my brother's funeral. I dipped into my basket, and I pulled out flower petals. I did it without my mother, I did it for my mother, and I thank God she didn't know.

Chapter Six

That's the beauty of Alzheimer's for my mother. Is there beauty to it? No, of course not, but of all the diseases in all the world, if she had to have one, better it be one that protects you from pain. She cried behind closed doors for a lifetime of pain that she did not know how to handle yet handled with grace. I truly believe that the events of 2007 would have killed her had she known of them.

While her youngest son lay dead on a bathroom floor from a grief too much to bear and a granddaughter eloped with a man and a cancer, she would have later heard the news reports. Most of Southern California was on fire. Her youngest daughter was being evacuated from those out-of-control fires. She then would have gone (if able) to be at her older daughter's side as she had a surgery for yet another cancer and recovery. Margaret was tough; however, she was alone by now, and she had been brave for so long through so much. Her mind was at rest. There were so many times when all I wanted to do was call my mother. Even though you know that she isn't available for one reason or another, if you have had the pleasure and the safe feeling of just hearing your mother's voice for most of your life, that is the first thing that pops into your mind. And every time that that happens you grieve for just a second before you move on. Margaret was not a woman full of wise words or even comforting ones, but she would always listen. I had crossed that bridge where you go from telling your mom all your woes to telling her almost nothing that would worry her long before the Alzheimer's. That did not mean that the urge, the dependency wasn't still in my heart.

I don't think my mother ever acknowledged her memory loss. She must have been frightened, concerned, frustrated, and depressed. On one of my family's visits I found a note with our arrival date and time in between her sofa cushions. She had been surprised and happy when we showed up at her door. Her husband, Hal, had moved them into a retirement home much to her chagrin; however, she had gone along with it, and his doing so had saved her kids a lot of trouble. Hal was gone now, and she had forgotten that she had ever lived anywhere else. She had forgotten that she had been married before Hal. How does one feel when your daughter shows up and surprises you with her visit, showing you a slip of paper that she says is in your handwriting, telling you of her arrival and then later in a feeble attempt at bonding breaks out the photo album and feebly attempts to convince you that a man in the picture book (the daughter's father) is/was your husband and you have *no* memory of it?

Margaret laughed, as she tells you "that man is not my husband, he is just another one of my good-looking boyfriends!" She laughs again and says she has paper like the paper the note is on, but that is not her handwriting.

She laughs and says regardless of feeling crazy she is glad that you are here! And you laugh with her because her laugh is infectious and has always been one of the biggest joys in your life. You try to keep laughing at all the weird and unusual things, but it's getting hard to laugh and harder still to not cry. And then you plan a trip, just a ride really. She has always loved to go for rides in the country. It'll be a long distance, an all-day trip, and she is aware of the distance and the time. My mother calls me in her bedroom and motions for me to sit beside her on the bed. I do. She tells me she can't go on the trip. She looks embarrassed, and I instantly know what it is. "Mom," I say slowly with great concern and care in my voice, "is it a bathroom thing?"

"Yes," she replies. She tells me she doesn't always make it in time. I ask her about Depends. Does she know of them? Is she comfortable getting them? She is. We go. We stop at lots of bathrooms, and we have a great time. It was our last *trip*.

The next time I visit my mom I come alone and on a mission. The retirement home has moved her from independent living to nursing care, and there is a problem. The nurse who is giving her morning medications is having a hard time getting her to take them. She has said that Mom has threatened her. Margaret threatened someone? I don't think so! I hate to fly. It terrifies me. But I do it all the time. It's part of life. The alternative is not an option for the way I want to live. I plan on staying for four days and three nights with my mom. I want to get a feel for her life, what she goes through, and how she goes through it. The first morning I awake to a nurse coming into the apartment with her key. She passes me on the sofa and walks into Mom's bedroom. I follow. She says loudly, "Wake up, Mrs. Wright. It's time for your medication." There's no response. She has always been a good sleeper. The nurse, who has already annoyed me, repeats her request. Mom turns over with a start. The nurse bends over my mother's body pulls the tangled white sheet from her face and neck, places her hand behind mother's neck, and pulled it toward the light of day and a glass of water. Mother reactively bats at the hand coming toward her, and the glass and water go flying across the bed toward the end, where it rolls off onto the floor. The nurse shrieks as she turns toward me and says, "She is always like this!"

Nurse Ratched has stormed out of the apartment, leaving the meds and a request for me to see to it that she gets her pills. I am horrified by the whole scene. My mother is now pacing the floor and saying things like this: "The nerve of that woman." I make an instant decision to give this woman the benefit of the doubt and allow her another chance to treat my mother with respect. It doesn't happen. The next morning is worse, and Mother, who was not startled on this morning but was annoyed that the woman did not knock on either the front or bedroom door, is loaded and ready when Ratched comes with her water glass and pills. Mom starts in on her right away, saying, "You come in here like you own the place every morning and force these pills that I don't even know what they are for at me when I am half asleep. Why can't you wait until I am awake?"

She had a point, and I called a meeting. I told the powers that be that this was a personality conflict at best and a lack of training at worst and that I wanted her removed from contact with my mom. I had not introduced myself to this nurse on my first morning because of her abruptness and my jet lag. It was only during the course of this meeting and then only in passing that I learned her first name was Mabel. I almost fell off my chair. Oh, that darn God sure has a sense of humor. Although Margaret presumably did not know of my father and my escapades, she was aware that when Dad ordered his beers and/or her drinks at any bar where he did not know the bartender, he always called them Mabel, which Mom found annoying and was somewhat jealous of his having a pet name for anyone other than her regardless of its generic intent. Was there more to this uncomfortable exchange between these two women? We'll never know, but I'm guessing the subconscious heart has no Alzheimer's.

My Aunt Pauline, Dad's sister, owned a bar named The Alibi, which I always thought was a clever name. I recently discovered a snazzy bar of the same name in Los Angeles. It bore no resemblance to Aunt Pauline's. Pauline's bar sat on a busy street not far from downtown Columbus and on the same street as her home. The front door was never used, but it faced the street. From the front door the bar trailed back from the street toward the side door. In between the front and side doors were about six small windows overlooking the parking lot. It was in this parking lot on this busy street that I fell asleep many a night in the backseat of our family car. I was not allowed to be up in the back window. I was to stay down where no one could see me. This wasn't because my parents thought they were doing anything wrong but so that no bad guys would see me and do something wrong. My dad would often carry me out to the car just before I was ready to drop from the time of night, too many Shirley Temples and too much game machine bowling.

Although Margaret hated Dad's affection for bars, she never objected to The Alibi and would always join him. Was this because Pauline was behind the bar as opposed to any Mabels? It confused the heck out of me at the time, but I think I have made sense out of it now. I often joke that I spent my childhood in a bar. I loved that place. My brothers both worked there for extra money. Tom had a particularly interesting and creative job. As soon as he was old enough to have a driver's license but not old enough to drink, he was given the assignment of gathering up the drunken troublemakers at The Alibi, offering to drive them down the street to the next bar where drinks would be on him. Money was supplied by Pauline. "Let someone else deal with the assholes," was her motto. I was no longer allowed in after the GoGo dancers of the 70s were brought in to pick up business. Just when it was getting interesting! Margaret may have enjoyed a cocktail or two; however, she didn't enjoy the GoGo dancers, and there went my days of game machine bowling. God, I missed that game. I was good at it.

Mom never drank much after those days. Once Mom didn't drink much, no one was supposed to drink much. The battle over the Christmas parties became the battle of daily life. Ironically that is when everything seemed to intensify as far as alcohol consumption was concerned. Dad started coming home from work, and after a brief stop at the fridge for a beer, he would head straight to the basement. He was working, and I never saw him not working down there; however, I also never saw him without a beer and a cigar down there. He enjoyed it. He was in his cave—safe like a mole from all things above ground, my dad the mole. If I wanted to see him, I had to go there and try to find something or some way to sit comfortably. I once asked him if I could bring a chair down for people (me) to sit in. "No," was his answer, and once my dad said no, there was no further discussion.

Wherever my dad was . . . was where I wanted to be. This never changed. If I am instructed by some New Age guru to go to my happy place, to this day I go to the front porch of the house in Columbus. It was a warm summer night just after the fireflies had begun rising from their slumber in the grasses. The streetlight three houses down from ours had a soft gold glow, and my father had the garden hose in his hand, watering the yard. I was not permitted to do this because "it is a precise science."

So I was content to sit beside him quietly as the frogs and crickets started to sing. His cigar smoke enveloped me, and he let me have one, maybe two sips of his beer. He would answer a question if I asked one, but I usually didn't have one. I got it. This was a time of peace.

I had a good childhood; however, this is the only peace that I ever remember. I have no doubt that it is why I can never drink a whole beer but enjoy sips and *love* the smell of cigars. Everyone left us alone out there. It seemed boring to them. I would ask him on more than on one occasion, "Why not use the sprinkler? Why do you wait until its dark? How can you see what you're doing?" It was magical, and they all missed it.

Magical nights and peace and quiet were not something my mom knew—at least not until the kids were grown and gone and she and Bill along with Mildred and her second husband, Charles, escaped the city to a little campground by a pond where they kept their perspective trailers side by side all year long. The gals would sometimes stay out in the woods all week; the men joined them on the weekends. They had many years of enjoyment out there until my dad passed away, and then Charles lost interest in going. This was permanent camping, and Margaret loved camping. She was a small-town girl at heart, and camping away from the big city appealed to her sense of peace, although the snakes she encountered did not. But they were the ground kind, not the kind I was always warned of.

My entire childhood my mother warned me of bad guys. They were around every corner, behind every fence, and looking in your windows. To my knowledge this wasn't because she herself had had any experience with bad guys. But she read every inch of the newspapers, and every night I would hear this sentence from her: "The paper is full of perverts again." Ironically I ran into bad guys all the time and have experienced in one way or another bad guys my whole life. So I am left with this question: Did my mother's overprotection/fear-mongering save and protect me or make me so paranoid that it caused me to suffer great battles with anxiety?

My first encounter with a bad guy was in first grade. It was 1961, so little girls wore dresses to school. I loved to swing on the giant sturdy swing sets of the school yard. They faced a field that led back to a housing development. You could swing either way—toward the school yard or the field. I chose the field as my mother always told me to keep my legs together and to tuck my dress closely to my body, even showing me how to accomplish this on our home swing set. I didn't love that set as the leg kept coming out of the ground (until Dad poured cement in) and making feel as though the whole set would topple over with me in it. When I sat toward the field, I didn't have to worry about any boys seeing up my skirt because as high as I wanted to pump my way to the sky I didn't want to worry about anything at all. I could fly in that swing and never think about anything at all except reaching for the clouds. I saw him every day, standing slightly behind the big tree halfway between the houses and the swing set. He didn't stay behind the tree; he was usually raking leaves that fall and nothing toward winter. He would end up behind the tree usually about the time I got to my maximize height on the swings. I would think about stopping and maybe telling someone that the guy behind the tree wasn't working, but that seemed a bit petty. The day he came toward me I stopped pumping my little legs so fast, and as he got closer, I began to let my feet scrape along the well-worn dirt under the swing to let myself slow down. He smiled, and I smiled. I thought he worked there. I thought everyone saw him. He started telling me that he liked my panties, something about their color. I felt panic.

I turned to find someone to help me. The playground was empty. The children were noisy, but the noise was faint and far. They had already started lining up at the doors to go in. In my panic I must have not heard the bell. This bad guy knew what he was doing. He had watched me for a long time; he knew my pattern from the time I hit the ground running to the swings, to the time I heard the bell to go back in. I always waited until the last kid lined up before I joined the line. I heard my name called. I turned to see not my first-grade teacher calling me, but my kindergarten teacher calling me from a distance that seemed much too far to save me. When I looked back, the bad guy was almost to his tree, where he had left his alibi, his rake. I told the teacher about the panties. Then I told the principal about the whole season of *raking*, but I had begged the teacher not to make me tell him about the panties. She didn't, but they called my parents and the police. I got to go home with my mom as my dad went back to work. That is the only time I remember my dad coming to my school. He looked livid, and my mom looked terrified. I never swung at that school again, and I may have stopped reaching for the clouds.

Chapter Seven

There were more bad guys that year and the years that followed, ones who offered me candy from their pockets if I reached in, one at the library, beating off in front of the space where he had removed just enough books for me to see his penis, and ones in cars that pulled over as I walked home from school, offering me everything from a ride to candy to the cliché holding of their fake puppy or kitten in the box on the backseat. I never told my mom or my dad about any of these. I did not want to see those looks that I saw the day of the reporting of the raker. I find it absolutely weird that all this and more happened to me as a kid. My mother warned me constantly about strangers, and as often as her warnings saved me, I wondered, *did this happen to other little kids? Why me?* I was cute, pale-skinned except in the summer, when I tanned easily, blond, usually curly from boxed *Toni* permanents, a bit skinny, and always cheery and pleasant, ready to comply, and therein lies my answer. Bad guys must see that coming a mile away—that and the naiveté.

The closest call remains a mystery and regret. School was over for the day, and the street in front of the school was lined for almost a block with cars full of awaiting parents and one bad guy. I was skipping out toward the street and was only in front of the third car when the door opened. A strange man leaned over nonchalantly and called my name. I stopped and fell about half a step toward his voice and open door. He smiled and said, "Hey, Christie, your mom can't make it to get you today, so she sent me for ya." I made one smaller step toward the open door, searching the backseat with my eyes. There were no boxes, but then he said, "She sent some cookies she made for our trip home." It was 1964. I guess bad guys assumed good moms made cookies. Except for Christmastime Margaret didn't bake cookies much.

I made a fast look down the row of cars. Bill had recently bought Margaret her first car. It was an embarrassment to me. It was old even for the sixties. It was a late 1940s Pontiac with a recognizable hood ornament, which even if you couldn't see that, you could spot its rounded and tall top above all the other more modern cars. That embarrassment most likely saved my life. I ran like the wind toward that car. Panting as I dove in the front seat, Margaret said, "Well, I am happy to see you too." I never told her until I was about thirty-five. God only knows what that man got away with, and God only knows how he knew my name. What? Was there some club where these pedophiles hung out and exchanged easy target information?

All the near misses of my elementary school days helped me a great deal when I hit puberty. Although still ready to please, I had developed quite the bad mouth for anyone who looked at me sideways, or whomever I deemed creepy. It caught them off guard when someone so sweet-looking unleashed loud, bad language toward them. They usually said something worse back and walked or sped away. This pretty much saved me until high school. I attended my brother's high school, Linden McKinley, which in a very short span of time had changed from a 90 percent white to a 90 percent black student body. Aside from a brief introduction to Margaret's fear-based prejudice the year before after my black friend, a boy named Steve, and I encountered some trouble in the record store, I did not know any prejudice. My parents did not vocalize any concern over Linden McKinley as I overheard others who did—that is, until the riots broke out. My parent's certainly were not racists. As my dad used to say, "Hell, I'm not prejudice, when I was a kid my cat's name was *Nigger,* he was black as night just like my best friend." I always thought my dad's childhood must have been like Huck Finn's; the way he threw around the word *nigger* like it meant nothing. He'd head for the sofa and say "Gotta watch Mitch [Miller] tonight "that Leslie Uggims is the best looking nigger I've ever seen." It makes me cringe now just like it did then. Margaret was disgusted by this as well, not with his choice of words mind you, but by yet another TV personality crush that he had. Meanwhile, I was under the radar as one of the only blonde gals at Linden McKinley, and it wasn't so much the guys who had me there. The girls at Linden, mostly African Americans, were nothing like any other girls I had ever met, and I found them utterly fascinating. In fact, I had never met any black girls. I found myself in a culture so much more assertive than my middle-class white-bread neighborhood; I gobbled up hanging with girls who seemed to know how to assert themselves in every situation in which I did not. Now in this new environment I was making fast girlfriends, one from homeroom and two from history class, and they were all three black. My only girlfriends in this high school were black. I had a friend named Debbie from junior high at first, but after she was attacked by a large gal with an umbrella as her weapon of choice, her parents quickly had Debbie transferred. The umbrella attacker was later expelled because she was apparently crazy. I had two friends in junior high school who were black boys. They to me were totally normal, typical boys, and by that I mean it didn't really cross my mind that they were any different from other teen boys. I realize now that they like me later at Linden were trying to fit in. Steve was the one I was with in the record department of Lazarus department store when my mother's fear-based prejudice had immerged. He and I were flipping through the albums when we were approached by three white boys our age. The first thing they said was, "Hey, nigger lover." I froze.

Steve looked ever-so-slightly up from the albums, turned slightly toward me, catching and holding my eyes, and said softly, "Don't say anything and don't turn around."

They spoke again, "Hey, we're talking to you, blondie, or should we say again . . . nigger lover . . . nigger lover?"

I turned, and I turned fast. I approached all three, and I got in their collective faces. And I said in my loudest, strongest voice, which is neither, "What did you say?" I knew that my words had no impact. What I had meant to be loud and intimidating had just come out more as if I didn't actually understand that, as if I had said, "Would you repeat that please?" I was shaking. My heart was pounding (I was sure visibly), and I had broken into a sweat. My future girlfriends at Linden would have handled this situation much better, and I would learn from them; however, this was where I was in space and time right now, and I had no tools for this. I felt Steve's hand grab my upper arm, and I heard him say not to me but to them, "We're leaving."

To which I replied to him and to them as I felt my anger building, "No, we're not. We are not."

Steve tightened his grip on my arm and said to the boys who were now stepping closer to us, "We're going."

I suddenly lost my attitude and realized it was three against two, actually one as I was girl and had begun visibly trembling. Whether it was from fear or anger I don't know, but I suspect both. When I got home that day, I felt high from my sense of unfairness and what I was going to do about it. I would start with my parents, and then they would help me inform Lazarus of this situation. And then I would get those boys banned from the store permanently. That was my plan. I had made Steve go with me to report the incident to security. All he wanted to do was get the hell out of there. I rode my bike as fast as I could all the way home, arriving breathless in the kitchen to tell my story to my mother. She stood there absolutely stunned. When I finished, I was the one banned. I was never to be in public with Steve *ever* again. My dad later told her that she was being unreasonable if this boy was my friend, but she was having none of it. Several years before, Billy and a coworker were jumped while they were waiting after dark at the bus stop. The coworker was a black kid. My mother banned Billy from the bus and the kid. My dad stepped in again, saying she was being unreasonable, and Dad started picking Billy and the coworker up from the night shift and taking them home. Billy had already been robbed at gunpoint during his night shift at Lawson's quick stop. It was too much for Margaret. It was as if the headlines were creeping into her life.

In the end they had reach a compromise in their minds although not in my mine. I could have Steve over after they met him, but I could not be out and about with him. Mom met Steve. We hung out, and all was well. So a funny thing happened on the way to the TV room a week after Mom met Steve. I brought home a bunch of kids to play Ping-Pong in the basement, which had turned into quite the rec room. One of the kids was another African American boy named Ron. Ron looked nothing like Steve. He was several inches taller and thinner, his skin tone as different as me in the summer compared to me in the winter, and he had no Afro like Steve had. Mom said, "Nice to have you back, Steve." God bless her. I was mortified.

Ron said, "I'm Ron, but we all look alike." God bless him. I never believed that my mom had been anything other than terrified for her children on these occasions. Prejudice was not what I believed about my mom until the Alzheimer's.

There are a lot of women of color who work in and with the elderly. In my mom's unit they are the majority. I have enjoyed and liked each and every person I have ever met there, save Mabel. And I appreciate all that they do for her and the other folks in this unit. They all have the patience of saints. I am famous for saying that my mom has never gone through an angry stage during her Alzheimer's. That is not entirely true. She was angry with her dipshit nurse back in the beginning stages of it, and she was angry with me during her withdrawal from antidepressants. And she was angry with an aid with dark skin and what Mom would have called jet-black hair, an aid who tried to get her to move to another chair. She called her a black-faced witch. I was there. I wanted to crawl under the nearest chair. I apologized, and then I cried. I cried because no matter what my mom ever felt or didn't feel about race she would have never said such a thing if she was in her right mind. Everyone knows that Margaret is a lady for God's sake. Apparently everyone but Alzheimer's knew.

I had heard many of the folks in her unit afflicted with this disease say horrible things to the workers, volunteers, each other, and their own families. I had never heard my mother speak in such a way. Where the hell did that come from? I never told a soul until now. Was it the disease? Was it some deep, hidden belief she had held down for so long? Was it just her frustration at her situation? Had she lashed out at someone with the only words that came to her mushed mind? Was my mom a racist? I have to go with no. I was never taught prejudice—period. I'm sticking with a woman who would at times in her life because of fear "react unreasonably," as my dad had said in the past. If the aid had been painted red, she would have called out, "Leave me alone, you red-faced witch."

A white kid named Rick threw some printed flyers over the balcony of Linden's auditorium during assembly. They basically said that the white kids were not getting the education that they should because the teachers were terrified of the black kids, and so they thought that nothing was being taught. The auditorium erupted in pandemonium. I wasn't there. I had gone home early because I had been teased at best and tormented at worst earlier in the day in the girl's bathroom. You had to have a hall pass to leave the classroom for any reason. I had my pass. The hall(s) were empty as was the bathroom. I was in the stall when I heard three or four girls come in and say, "You in here, blondie? We have scissors, and we are gonna cut off all that pretty blonde hair of yours. Come out, come out wherever you are."

After I gave them fair warning, I screamed, and they left.

I had been in sticky situations before at Linden. Once a girl and her two cohorts slammed my arm inside my locker and said if I ever looked at her man again she'd cut me, and then she showed me the very small pocketknife. I had no idea who her *man* was. A girl who sat beside me in homeroom and with whom I had past back and forth a few notes came to my rescue, simply telling these thugs to go away and "leave her alone." Another time a couple of gals in history class drilled me on what I would do if a black boy asked me out. I said, "If he was cute, I'd go." They laughed, nodded, and later in the week saved me when I was jumped in the gym by yet other girls who said I was after one or the other's man. I never told my parents about any of this. But everyone could feel the tension building at school between the races. I had walked to school in the beginning, but now my mom picked me up every day, looking terrified. I never overheard my folks talk about it though, so either they didn't talk about the issue, or more likely they were discreet. So when I came walking home that day before *the riots*, my mom went into action. She didn't buy my "I started my period" story (which was true). She knew by the way moms know things that something was off with me. The bathroom girls had scared me. It was a hair thing. I thought my hair looked like Peggy Lipton's from the television show *Mod Squad*, and I was terrified of losing it. My life goal was to look like Peggy Lipton.

I never went back to Linden, and I missed it. Long before Rodney King spoke through the media words that so many of us have thought so many times, I felt the whole "can't we all get along" challenge. At my new school (we moved to a new neighborhood) the only challenge was this: "Can't we all wear cute clothes." I missed my childhood home, my childhood neighbors' young an old, and all my old haunts. I became depressed. I knew a lot of the kids there from junior high; however, I had lost touch with friends from then, and my grades went down. I felt lost, unchallenged in the way I liked and still like to be challenged. There was some truth to Rick's flyers. I knew of at least two teachers whose classrooms were completely out of control, and if you just showed up for attendance, you could score an A. But there were good teachers and good students I missed. I kept in touch with my homeroom friend for a little while; however, then her parents took her out of Linden as well, and I made new friends as I'm sure she did. My boyfriend from junior high also left Linden as his dad told the district that either they let him transfer out of Linden (they had no intention of moving) or his son would be quitting school. Parents of all students regardless of race were desperate.

I was on my best behavior after that. I just wanted to get through high school and get out in the world on my own and see it all. I was turning quite shy and withdrawn and felt as if I were always on edge. Everyone at this school seemed so much smarter, better-looking, and more mature than I was. There were a lot of kids smoking pot, dropping acid, and having sex, none of which I wanted to do. I became obsessed about two things after that: dying and getting pregnant. I would never do anything that would cause either of those things to happen. I had nightmares about both. Usually I was pregnant, and the baby died inside me. It was horrible, and I couldn't sleep through most of high school. Mom didn't seem to pick up on any of this. I didn't cut, but I picked at my fingers with safety pins. Unlike cutting, which one tries to hide, I wanted someone to notice my fingers. I began using my hands to talk, especially with Mom. If anyone did notice, nothing was ever said. Maybe that was denial.

I had seen a lot of death and dying as a young person. The first funeral that I attended was for Mary Ann, my childhood friend. Mary Ann was the oldest kid on our block. She was beautiful with long dark hair and big blue eyes. She had the longest lashes I had ever seen. She was so pure, never engaging in any of the wicked kid games we could come up with. She died because she had had an epileptic seizure in a lake at a summer camp. She was Catholic. I was not, but I was a Catholic wannabe as I attended mass with my next-door neighbors often and just loved the incense, the covering of your head, the Virgin, the holy water, and the candles. God, I loved the candles. Our Lutheran church was so boring by comparison. Plus where was the Virgin in my church? Once I saw her, I never wanted to turn away from her beauty. Mary Ann lay in her coffin of pale blue silk peacefully with her curled dark locks arranged around her face and shoulders and the rosary entwined gracefully between her delicate, manicured fingers. Flower arrangements of roses, lilies, and a whole bunch of others I didn't know the names of surrounded her, almost taking her over. If I had to die, this is how I was going, with those beads around my hands and all those flowers.

There were a lot of other funerals of relatives that I did not really know, old people who looked scary in their coffins. My uncles had begun to die too. One by one they got cancer or had heart attacks. It was always very sad, and everyone seemed so at a loss. I was getting used to funerals. It was part of life. Then a little girl whom I had walked to kindergarten every day for her first year of school (it was my first babysitting job) was electrocuted in her blow-up swimming pool over the summer break. I was only ten years old. It was beyond my comprehension. I had to continue to walk past her house every day of school for the next three years. Only once did I see her mother, and she did not speak to me. Even at my young age I understood that it was too painful to acknowledge me. I loved that little kid, and she knew it. I felt such deep sorrow for that loss, and I wanted to tell her mom that day I saw her in the yard. But I walked past—only to fantasize for the rest of that year. In my dream I would walk up tall and brave to their front door and knock, and when her mom opened the door, we would gaze into each other's eyes. And then I would just hold her. It never happened.

There was a break in deaths after a while and before my dad's broke my heart. I had gone to the Grand Canyon for a vacation and ended up going back to work there when I turned twenty-one. I made friends fast. One friendship was with a wild girl named Kathy with a taste for adventure. She seemed so alive, wanting to party all night, and she seemed to literally dance all day. Every step I saw her take she took with a leap of faith. She had made friends with a shady character, a Native American guy who none of the local Navajos or Hopis knew. He had just shown up one day with good pot. She told us all that she and he were hitching to Flagstaff and she asked if we wanted to go. I had only hitched twice, once out of adventure and once out of necessity. I had no intention of doing it again. Besides, this guy was a little strange. Her friend that she had come to the canyon with had to work, and no one else seemed interested either. We all ended up regretting our decisions.

We all were interrogated by the sheriff's office after they had been missing for five days. I knew my interrogator; he had been trying to get me on a date for months. I thought it would be easy; however, he was very serious about it, and it made me very nervous. I felt like I was going to pass out before it was over. We all thought this guy whom Kathy had gone off with had murdered her and taken off in search of his next victim. We thought that until both of their bodies were found buried in shallow graves off Highway 180 between Flagstaff and the turnoff to the Grand Canyon.

My mom was right. There were bad guys, and there were bad things. And none of this was helping me stop dreaming of death and destruction. My anxiety, which had begun as a child, was starting to disrupt my life just like I had watched it disrupt my mother's. It was more than just a lack of desire for reaching for the clouds. I didn't want to reach outside my front door. I was retreating inside myself, shutting down, and checking out. I found out in therapy in my thirties that it actually has a name, a term. After several panic attacks, one leaving me curled up in a fetal position and unable to straighten out because of the contraction of every muscle in my body, I began what was to become twelve years of therapy. That's when I found out that I had been checking out since I was a little girl. My therapist called it dissociative personality disorder. It had protected me for a long time. Did I really want to give that up and join the real world? And another bigger question was this: Had this been my mom's problem, her disease? Was Alzheimer's an extension of this if you never figured it out and fixed it, healed it? Were denial and checking out cousins?

I was worried about my mental health after Lacey was born. I had been told by my medical doctor that I had postpartum depression. During my pregnancy with Lacey I had mood swings and was sick every morning of my first trimester. Although I continued to work full-time through my pregnancy, it was terribly difficult to get through each day. Edema had also become a problem. During my C-section I had a panic attack, but I didn't realize it until I had another nine months later. Lacey had been pulled from my womb and was having her eyes wiped for her presentation to me, when I heard a nurse asked about the surgical rags. Apparently they were not all accounted for. I heard counting; one, two, three, four, five, and so on up to seventeen, and then I heard my doctor say, "I'm going back in." I felt the pressure down low and then the pressure of a hand or hands inside me all the way up to under my ribs. I turned my head toward Mark at my right side to ask what was going on as everything in my head seemed fuzzy. He was looking down at what was going on and not paying attention to me at all. I then turned my head to my left toward the anesthesiologist and asked the same question. She had been so kind in explaining to me what was going to happen pre-op and held my hand through it all. Now she let go of my hand, touched my brow ever-so-gently, and said something about morphine to someone other than me as she told me that I should relax my breathing and that everything was okay. I know now that I was hyperventilating—something that I would continue to do for the next decade.

In the waiting area a very nervous grandma said that she knew this. "Something is wrong." Mark's mother, Phyllis, had always been intuitive.

Another very nervous grandma Margaret told Phyllis, "Please don't say that." Margaret would tell me after that she couldn't believe that woman would say such a thing at such a time. Later when Margaret took my baby in her arms, she lit up with joy, and the two souls seemed to meld together. I've never seen anyone, myself included, look more at ease with a baby in their arms.

Seeing that was what helped me to relax. I had had an allergic reaction to the morphine and could not stop shaking. I didn't know either in the operating room or the recovery room what had happened. I was in an altered state of mind both from panic and drugs, and no one had bothered to clue me in. I believe that if either, Mark, my doctor, or anyone in that room had bothered to tell me, "Hey, we misplaced a rag, but it's cool. We're just going back in to find it," I would not have felt panic. This had been the constant in my life, the unknown that would send me over an edge. I never trusted the process of life.

Lying in my hospital bed that night with my newborn and my husband in my room, I knew that I would never be the same. Fear filled my head, while pure joy lifted my heart. I held my child to my breast, and I knew why I was on this earth. I also knew what I had always known about motherhood, it was terrifying and completely and utterly fulfilling. I would have to be brave. I had had a great teacher in Margaret. Years later as I sat with my therapist complaining about Margaret's lack of attention (forgetfulness) to birthdays, Christmas gifts, and phone calls, most especially to my daughter, neither I nor my therapist knew very much about Alzheimer's.

Chapter Eight

Margaret had been driving to Newark to take her turn tending to Mary for a year. It had worn her out physically, emotionally, and mentally. Mary had begun showing signs of *senility* and dementia after her last living brother, Ted, had died. They had been a family of eight kids. All Mary's girls, son, and daughter-in-law were exhausted. It was time to get help. They all agreed to have her "put in a home" where she would receive round-the-clock care. It was also agreed that all the kids would be present when the driver and caregivers from the home showed up to pick up Mary. Mary did not go willingly, and Margaret was the only one present. Mary yelled at Margaret, telling how much she hated her for this and how she would never forgive her. Mary had been yelling and hating for a while now, but it was somewhat evenly dispensed and mixed in with times of sweetness. This was ugly. The kids were told that there was to be a period of adjustment and that they should stay away for two or three days. They believed what they were told. Meanwhile, Mary's head was shaved, and she was dunked in a large bath while she was screaming. This was the nineties. It never crossed anyone's mind that this would be a practice anywhere. Mary died within days. She was ninety-four and in otherwise good health. Margaret never got over it.

In 2004 Margaret's sons picked her up to take her to a home. She yelled at them. She looked at Billy, whom she had spoiled and asked, "And you . . . you agree with this?" He said that he was sorry but that he did. Billy had done so much for her since our father had died. He had mowed her grass weekly, taken her rides monthly and would even come at the drop of a hat to remove a spider for her. I believe she was very shocked that he would decide to stop doing for her and just put her in the care of others. I was not there. Brenda was not there. Hal had passed away. He had done us a great service when he talked her into moving from her home to a retirement home with him the year before. That was the big move, the one she would have never done if not for his wishes. We had all packed up her home. There had been an estate sale, donations to The Salvation Army, and a rented trash bin out front. I had done most of the closets and basement. She didn't remember most any of that stuff, so I stayed out of trouble with her. I threw out trash bag after trash bag of cut-out recipes and craft articles that had been saved in piles up to the rafters. I took at least a hundred shoe boxes of old and new holiday cards and craft supplies to local churches. I had already discovered the upside of Alzheimer's. You can sneak a lot of bullshit by them. She hadn't been in her basement in a long time, at least since her fall. Hal had been doing the laundry down there. She just didn't remember what was down there.

Margaret had a very hard time finding her way around the halls of her new home with Hal, but he always took her hand and led her, so there was no need for her to pay attention. After he died, she got lost on her way to the dining hall and the recreation room for movie night every time. When I would visit, I stayed close to her. If I wanted to see friends, I invited them there. My good friend Robin came several times. It was here that I had stayed on for three days, determining the problem with the nurse. It was here that Donna and I made the decision to begin to lessen her choices of clothing options as dressing had begun to stress her out. My mom always dressed well. I mentioned the heels and the lipstick as her staples. Now she used the lipstick on her cheeks, and she sometimes chose two different heels. Upon noticing any of this, she always laughed at herself.

Our best laugh in those days of the early stages was when she caught me in her closet in the middle of the night. I went in the walk-in, turned on the light, closed the door ever-so-gently so as not to wake her, and began sorting through her clothes, trying to narrow her choices down to easily matched colors. As I said I had learned that with Alzheimer's you could get away with a lot. Much to my surprise the door swung open and we both stood screaming at each other, not so different from the scene in the movie *ET* when Drew Barrymore finds ET in the closet. We burst out laughing, both apologizing for scaring the crap out of each other. She then turned and went back to bed. She had no idea why I was in her closet, and I had no idea why or how she had awoken at 2:00 a.m. and found me there.

Another time occurred when she had forgotten to put her bridge in when we out for breakfast. She realized it when the food arrived at our table. She had already asked if she liked butter on her pancakes. She loved butter. Our family joke was that if your name was Larason you put butter on your food. She didn't like pancakes, but she thought she should try pancakes as they sounded good. Nothing was mentioned the morning after the closet scare or at any other time these *funny* episodes occurred. I went on to do the closet task many times over. When the boys moved her into the new home, the Alzheimer's unit of Knightsbridge in Upper Arlington, the luxury of a walk-in was no more, and much condensing was needed. By then although still a well-dressed woman, she could no longer remember any of her clothes, but she could chose well from what she saw. One of the largest obstacles to overcome for families in this situation is how to handle folks stealing each other's clothes—or as we began to fondly call it, "shopping." They go into any closet they can and put on whatever they find. The staff finds it challenging to do laundry and get everything in its rightful home, so labeling is recommended. It is shockingly sad when you realize how appalled you are to see your loved one in someone else's clothes, usually something that he or she would normally never wear. Once you realize how much this does not matter, you are halfway to accepting joining the Alzheimer's world. The journey to this halfway point has felt like being blindfolded and being led into a place, an existence to which you have no intention of going, let alone go willingly. You are kicking and screaming. And what about the one with the disease? That person has never needed you more to just go along than he or she does now, but there is nothing harder than joining someone who is losing his or her mind. But that is what you must do because that loved one can no longer stay in your world.

The males of my family always said my mom was stubborn. My mom was not always right, but she always believed that she was right. It was her way or the highway. My dad seemed to have no problem with it being her way. If he did, he retreated to the basement, delayed his arrival at home with varies Mabels, or just didn't speak. My brothers argued with her constantly. They foolishly believed they could get her to see that west was east. They couldn't because in her mind she knew and they were just plain wrong. Brenda and I argued with her a bit but usually ended up laughing with her. I admired that she stuck to her guns. I did not see this as stubbornness. I saw it as tenacity. And I saw a big difference between obstinacy and firmness. Margaret was firm.

I do not know if Mom ever knew that she had a memory problem. There is a stage of Alzheimer's where you start making up excuses for your lapses. She was very good at making up those excuses. She also had a great sense of humor over her memory faux pas. I knew that she knew something was amiss when she pulled me aside to explain the snowballs on her Christmas tree. Although she knew what she was doing, she also knew that she didn't always; hence, she knew that we were wondering if she had lost it.

Her first official visit to be tested for Alzheimer's was one of the worst days of my life with her. She was so nervous and did not understand why she was going to this new doctor or what she was going for; however, by this stage of this horrific game, she had begun to go along to get along. The very kind and patient doctor began giving the test: "Remember these five things. Spell this backwards." By the time he got to the art and the math, she was full of panic. She had never been able to do math and swore that she could not draw a straight line. Just past that came what should have been easy.

"What is your full name?"

"Margaret Wright," she said.

"What is your middle name?"

Mom had no way out of this—not humor, not excuses, not firmness, not stubbornness. She did not know her middle name or even if she had one. But she was so brave that she did not buckle, she did not crack, and she simply folded her hands and put them calmly in her lap and said, "I guess I fail—"

I couldn't bear it, so I didn't.

I broke in and said, "Of course not. You don't know your middle name because you hate it. You've always hated it, and so you forgot it. You've put it out of your mind!"

The kind doctor smiled at me. Mom's shoulders relaxed. My sister-in-law's uneasy laugh filled the silence. My forlorn-looking mother asked, "What is it?"

"It's Francis. It's Margaret Francis," I replied with a great big smile on my face.

"Oh, I don't like that very much."

We all laughed, and the test continued with little pain and more laughter. But there was the confirmed diagnosis of Alzheimer's by the end, and there was no more laughter.

At some point after that day Mom was put on antidepressants. The explanation was that everyone in the unit was on them. They had Alzheimer's, and they were depressed. Alzheimer's and depression go together like salt and pepper. My problem with that is that I don't like pepper. She did not seem depressed to me, but maybe she didn't remember that she was depressed. It's a tricky situation. But hey, she was old. She was in her eighty's now, and what was so wrong about a few happy pills? The problem was that once a person in her position was put on these, that person was never taken off them. It made life and work a hell of a lot easier for the staff. Don't get me wrong. I'm all for what gives these angels of mercy better days, but my grievance is with families who do not monitor their loved ones.

Mom could not stay awake. Some of this was normal and just one of the stages playing out. Some of this was because she and others were being overdosed. Mom was on several medications—everything from blood pressure meds to water pills for edema. Brenda also wanted her on many different vitamins. It was very hard to get these folks to take medications. They didn't know what the pills were or why they are taking them. They were in various stages of the disease and might at times think the nurse was trying to kill them. They were not children and did not want to be forced into anything, including eating, much less pill taking. I was not comfortable with the amount of struggle Mom's meals had become, mostly because of the pill-popping. While I understood that Brenda's insistence on Mom taking vitamins came from love and concern, I didn't agree with it. It was just too uncomfortable for Mom and too difficult for the nurse. The last thing that you want to do to someone with Alzheimer's is scare them. Taking pills that are forced upon you is scary, especially when you don't know who is forcing them on you, even if it's the same person as yesterday. You don't remember yesterday. What you may remember though is you don't like this person.

The one thread of sanity that I always held on to when I was visiting Mom was that she always seemed to know that I was someone she loved. This lasted until nine years into this disease. I always felt that I could make her smile, even laugh at times. Even after she began to speak gibberish, I felt I could still do so because I knew her personality and I could hold a conversation with her. I could pick out a certain word or name from her gibberish and go along with her, laughing when she did, agreeing as she would want me to, and saying yes in the appropriate spots by watching her body language. She trusted me. She also trusted me to feed her, although like all those afflicted, she sometimes rejected the offering. So when she did not allow me to give her any pills, I felt that we really needed to revisit what she was taking.

Brenda was not on this page with the rest of us. We asked her to at least come to a meeting that I would arrange with the house doctor. She agreed and I asked for the meeting. The house doctor was a man who attended to all the patients in the unit. He and his nurse checked blood pressure, looked in eyes and up noses, checked feet and legs for swelling, and not much else. No one in the history of Knightsbridge or his stint at this current career situation had ever asked to meet with him before I did. Not one single family member of all the folks who had passed through the doors of this unit had ever met with this man! After I made the call to Sandy, she in turn called his office. We learned shortly thereafter that he not only did not want to meet with us but was extremely curious and apprehensive of our motive.

The day we met we entered the *meditation room* of the unit. Ironically it was never used for intended meditation, but it is very calming. There were two overstuffed sofas of muted green floral, each covered with matching pillows with fringed edges and soft throws layered on the backs. In between the sofas a dark walnut table hosted a replica of an old-time radio that usually played a big band or classical CD. This room was nestled in the middle of the unit, so the windows on two sides, one viewing the hall and one the dining area, give a distressing view of folks walking and/or pacing the halls. There are two large French doors that are never closed. For viewing and calming pleasure there is a large aquarium on the one solid wall. It is usually kept darkened, the only light coming from the soft bulb in the table side lamp. It is a nice room. This day it was set up for our meeting. There were a few extra chairs placed, and the doors were freed to be closed upon our arrival. It was in this calming place that the house doctor accused me, my sister, and my sister-in-law of trying to *off* my mom for money.

Chapter Nine

Margaret did not like dealing with money. Money involved numbers, and numbers meant math. Bill had handled the money in their marriage. He gave her cash for groceries each week. She had a Lazarus credit card for anything that she wanted there. When that bill came, as it did each month, Bill paid it without question or comment. But that was it for her. Anything outside of that he pulled from his wallet. She would sometimes say that she needed more grocery money, meaning she needed something other than what could come from either the Big Bear or Lazarus.

After Bill passed away, our mother turned her checkbook over to Tom, and he put the account in his and her names. Things changed a bit as she would now go to the bank to withdraw any cash that she may need and she would write her own checks; however, she had Tom do the balancing. Margaret never had gotten over her lack of a full education. She had taken some craft classes in her adult life but never any education classes of any kind.

She was stuck with what she had learned as a child and had no interest in learning anything more than that. "I can't do math. I just can't." Each one of her children heard this during their school years. Any Larason kid who required simple help with arithmetic homework was sent straight to our dad. Her fear of money and/or numbers didn't just end there. It extended itself into odd places.

Margaret liked money, the bills themselves. She wanted new bills, and she wanted them always in her possession. She had been this way since she was a kid. As a very young girl she knew that she wanted to make her own money. She wrote her name and address on several small sheets of paper and decorated them with little drawings of flowers and trees. "I wish I still had those," she told me in one of late-night talks. "I couldn't draw a straight line now. I bet those were pretty silly trees and flowers on those notes!" She took them around town, dropping them in mailboxes or tucking them away inside screen doors of front porches. The latter didn't last long as her delivery method after a dog jumped at the screen door. Her next-door neighbor hired her at the tender age of nine to do her ironing. It was on this, her first official job that she realized that you could iron a bill almost to look as if it were a new one! Each week after she was paid, she would save the money till the next week so that she could iron the previous week's pay after the neighbor's clothes were done.

My mom sat of the sofa and told me this story about her first job with that faraway look that she would get whenever she reminisced. When I asked her why it was important to her that the money look new, she said softly, "My dad only ever had crumpled, dirty-looking money, and he gave it to men who looked that way too." I don't know how she came about her job as a speakeasy lookout. The ironing job had developed into a higher-paying job with more responsibility after two years. She was to be present when the neighbor's children came home from school. Her job was to see to it that they got a snack and then occupy their time until the mistress of the house came home from her own job. Margaret loved babysitting those three kids, ages six, seven and nine. She kept doing this even after the family could no longer pay her for babysitting, much less any ironing or other chores.

Everyone had heard that Mom was a lookout for a speakeasy. It was Bill's favorite story, but if you asked Margaret about it, it never happened. I know that she felt ashamed by it, and no matter what was said, you could not get her to see the humor in it, much less how interesting it was. I asked her privately once if it was true.

"It's true, but I'll never admit it. And I never kept that money for myself."

"What did you do with it?" I asked.

"I gave it all to my mom."

"What for?" I inquired. We were having a moment of complete honesty that I had only dreamt of!

"I just knew she needed it."

"Where was this place?" I asked.

"It was in a basement."

"Whose?"

And that was the end of the conversation. She looked at me sideways, put up her hand as if to say, "Enough," and picked up the paper that she had been reading before I had entered the living room and sat on the sofa beside her. I have often wondered if I would have ever gotten the story out of her. I had been jaded too many times by my dad to ask him what he knew. In actuality, I don't believe that he knew any more than what I found out because no one seemed to go past the point of the story that said Margaret was a lookout for a speakeasy, as if to imply, "Isn't that something?"

Margaret thought money was dirty. When my grades began to slip, Dad wanted to pay me for A's. This caused an argument the likes of one which I had never seen or heard before. No way was that going to happen. She knew that she could not help me get A's. Not in math anyway, which is where I was slipping. This paying for grades was dirty business, and it would set her and me up for failure. Bill, who was pretty good at numbers, just thought I needed to apply myself. I, on the other hand, thought if they would take the letters out of the *new math*, I'd be fine, but I was completely thrown off by this *new math*. Margaret won, and I never did understand algebra until my daughter helped me when I was in my forties and had gone back to school.

I thought that my mom would be thrilled that I was going to go to college. I had spent many a day trying to win the approval of my mother. As it turned out I had the approval of no one. Mark had been playing music for the Four Seasons, which had led to an opportunity to travel to South Korea to headline for the opening of the Ritz-Carlton there. It was a lot of money and a lot of time, six months. Lacey was in second grade, and I had already gone through a scary process of both matriculation and explanation to my young daughter about what I was going to be doing during the day. I was determined to at least start college. I didn't care how long it took me to get through. The Ritz offer came after that fact, and Mark expected me to drop what I was doing, as was the pattern of our marriage and go to Seoul, South Korea, with him and Lacey for six months. It wasn't going to happen. I thought that our disagreement was over him staying, and he thought it was over me going. When I finally realized that he was bound and determined to go, I made us an appointment for marriage counseling. I had thrown myself on our bed in convulsions of tears, begging him not to go. He was going to go, and although I understood that as a husband and father he felt this was something that he had to do to make a lot of money for our family, I knew he would have hell to pay from me. I would be resentful. I would work on it, but it would happen. He was disregarding my opinion and my feelings, which was even more hurtful. We needed to go and get a plan in place to work through the impending hell I would no doubt put him through.

Margaret was beside herself with this news. She could not understand how I could understand or how he could disregard my feelings. It was the first time that she was upset with her son-in-law since he had become that to her. She said that she would come out to stay with me for as long as she could to help with Lacey so that I could carry on with my plans, but she also said that I shouldn't really be going to school at my age and with a young child and now an absent husband. I wasn't thrilled with news that help was on the way. My mom had been of great help to me as an adult many times, most notably during a bout with a blood clot. But that was when my dad was alive. Now Margaret was with Hal, and he was trying to say the least. I knew that he would not allow her to come alone. Mom had been such a blessing to have around after Lacey was born. She was so amazing with her and with me. They had a very special relationship as Margaret had with all of her grandchildren. I knew this would be a great time for the two of them if Hal didn't interfere.

Mark left for Korea, and I began college. Lacey started second grade, and Mark wrote letters of woe being all alone here in this foreign land with nothing but room service at the Ritz-Carlton. I dealt with the rain damage of El Nino, Lacey with pneumonia, lack of study skills at forty years old, my job, and the pets. By the time Margaret and her new husband arrived, I was in full-on panic-attack mode. I wasn't the only one. Lacey had also had a panic attack on the playground of her school. I was one of the volunteers that day, so I was there to recognize it for what it was and get her through it. While that was a saving grace, I was horrified as I knew it was more my fault than anyone's. I was the one who had thrown myself on the bed, thrashing in screams and pleading as if it were the end of the world right in front of my daughter.

Hal wanted to wait until after the rains had stopped (which wasn't going to ever happen that year). They waited. Lacey got very ill, missing three weeks of school, and I got by with the help of my good friends, neighbors, and a very understanding boss. By the time they were due in town I was so full of resentment, fear, and longing that the thought of their arrival caused a most unusual occurrence in one of my classes. I was taking a test that I had studied well for. I sped through it, finished first in the class, and left for the airport to pick them up. I was a nervous wreck. The next time I attended that class the tests were given back to us, and I saw that I had failed. I had been doing well in college. In fact, my dad would have gone broke. After class I approached the professor's desk and asked if I could see the test again. She had read the questions in class with all of us, and we had gone over the correct answers. It had multiple-choice and true-and-false questions. She agreed and said that she was going to ask to speak with me anyway. As it turned out I had answered each question the opposite of the correct answer. In other words each true I had answered false and vice versa, and for each multiple choice I had answered the obvious incorrect answer. I started to cry. At forty years old I began to weep like a baby. This wonderful woman brought me a chair, told me to breathe, and said, "I knew you knew these answers and I noticed the strange pattern of the test answers. I'll give it to you again if you can take it right now." That time I passed. Pressure put on ourselves can cause such unbelievable stress on our minds.

It was during this visit with my mom that I decided I had to clear the air about my childhood. I needed to get my act together, and this seemed like where I should start. Margaret's memory had never been very good. I knew this would be a challenge to get her to remember anything that bothered me, let alone acknowledge that she may have failed me in any way and then get an apology. I was taking on a lot, and the timing wasn't great. Going to college and finding out that I was smart, not the dumb blonde that I had grown to believe I was because of the whole math setback, had empowered me. I was ready to take her on.

We talked for over an hour. She did what she did best, she listened. She always listened, she just never heard. It was always hard for her to pay attention. I told her that I loved her, that I knew she loved me, but that being raised to be seen and not heard was damaging. I spoke of how being the youngest and perhaps the most sensitive and yet being ignored left no room for self-esteem. I came after the lessons the parents had learned from the others; therefore, I got nothing that had been tried before. She listened as intently as she could. Only a few times did her eyes glaze over and her attention drift. Then she did the most amazing thing. She asked me for an example! I gave her one, namely the first time that I had thrown myself on a bed and wallowed around in screaming terror, pleading to not be left alone with Billy as my babysitter but to call Kathy from next door. Again my mother amazed me. "Why didn't I?"

I was so stunned. I replied with the only thing I had available to my memory: "I don't think she was home." We both found this very funny and laughed so much that the banished Hal and Lacey came to see what the fuss was all about.

When it was all said and done, my dear mother said, "Christie, I don't remember any of these things that you are talking about, but they must be true, so I am sorry."

There it was; all that I needed.

I cannot help but think that Margaret recognized her own childhood feelings in mine. She, too, was the ignored child, the youngest girl and sensitive. We had a lovely visit. One day before they were due to fly home, we walked along the beach, and we held hands, a rare thing for us. She told me that she didn't want to leave but that Hal needed to go home. I told her to stay but knew that she would go with her man. She told me that she was proud of me for being so brave through all that had been going on. I wanted to say so much, tell her it was nothing, that she was the brave one. Mostly I wanted to tell her that I wished she could feel what I was feeling from going to college. I wanted so much for her to feel the empowerment of learning again.

I noticed a lot about my mother during this visit, but I couldn't put my finger on what was different about her. There was an acceptance of life that she had never had before. She had come into my kitchen a few days after she and Hal had arrived, and she told me to hold out my hand and close my eyes. Again this was weird for her, for us. She wasn't big on surprises. In my hand she placed a ring. It was the cameo that Bill had given after they had first been married. I had told her when I was pretty little that I loved that ring and I'd really love if she wanted to put it in her will for me! I felt so forward, so inappropriate, and uncomfortable, but you should see this ring. When I opened my eyes and saw what it was, I looked up at her in disbelief. Margaret gave nothing away, ever.

"I know," she said. "I wanted you to have it before I forgot that you wanted it." I thought at the time that was just a figure of speech, something someone would say who was aging and realizing that they didn't need to hold on to everything any longer. What I have since come to see in so many of the things that she said after that day and that ring was a series of confessions of a fear that she was losing her ability to hold on to thoughts, memories, and promises.

There was never time during my mother's fall into loss that I paid attention to any signs of memory. I know this sounds strange. Brenda paid nothing but attention to our mother's memory. My sister had been the memory keeper for our family. She spent years putting together photo albums and labeling each picture with names, dates, and places. The first time that we ever began to reminisce by looking over these albums was one of the first times that we found out Margaret didn't remember Bill. She just couldn't figure out who that man in the picture (with her) was. Brenda, Lacey, Mom, and I all sat down together in Mom's TV room (my old bedroom). It was a small room that only fit a small sofa bed and a chair with the TV opposite. Its walls were still the blue that I had wanted them painted, but this room never meant anything to me. It was just a stop over until I could move away from home. As we all got lost in each of our photo albums in our laps, Lacey had lots of questions about who was who. She would hold up her album for us and ask, "Who is this baby? Who is that baby? Is that so-and-so? Where was this taken?" I had a lot of answers. Brenda did some hemming and hawing before answering, and Mom would just wait to see what everyone else said. Brenda would pressure her. "Mom, look at it. You know who this is, right?"

At one point Lacey had asked about a baby photo, and her grandma perked right up and said, "Well, that's Brenda, of course." Lacey looked at me, doubtful of the answer. I shook my head at her and put my finger to my lips in the shhhh gesture. Did it really matter that the picture was of me and not Brenda? Not at all. All that mattered was that her baby's pictures, just like her babies and all babies brought a smile to her lips.

It was during this quiet time together that I learned for the first time that my baby book I now held in my lap had not one word written in it by my mother. There were words, firsts of this or that baby accomplishments, but I came to find out Brenda had filled them all in. I was delighted and deflated—delighted that my big sister had taken the time as a teenager to see to this task, thereby giving me this gift, deflated that my mother had not done it. Margaret had carefully filled in all the firsts for those kids born four years apart. This began a round of "she always liked me best," a joke my sister and I had always played. We continued to play well into our mom's descent into the hell of Alzheimer's. We would visit Mom together, and upon seeing us, she would react or not react depending on the time of day, her state of mind, be it sleepy, drugged, or dazed for any number of reasons. My toothy smile, which I always showed whenever I entered any space Margaret occupied, usually won me the "she always liked me best" first round. Brenda's attentiveness to Mom physically by always touching her usually made her the second-round winner as Mom would start to talk. Then we would tie as we continued to feed her mind and occupy her time with picture books that I had made and Brenda had bought as well as tons and tons of magazines. No one was trying to teach her anything or get her to remember anything. Margaret loved magazines. There was always a subscription or ten in her house. *Better Homes and Gardens*, *Ladies Home Journal*, *Family Circle*, *Reader's Digest*, and later as her mind turned to mush, so did her magazines, the *National Enquirer*, *The Globe*, etc. We tried to find ones with lots of baby pictures. I made a large scrapbook with large pictures of adorable babies. I would win our game when we got to that as Margaret would smile and laugh and comment on the cute babies. Once she had gone through it the first time, she would start it all over. Another upside was that each picture was another adorable baby that she had not seen just minutes before.

That particular book lasted all the way though Margaret's disease. The small hardcover books that Brenda bought of babies (both human and animal) lasted as well. What didn't last was looking through magazines. There came a point when Mom just tore up the pages because of her lack of finger/hand control. She didn't seem to even know what she was doing. It would just happen. We gave up on magazines. We would have to find another way to both entertain her and ourselves when we were with her. I learned from Lacey that being goofy was a great source of joy for Mom. I had forgotten that. Lacey was deeply sad that her grandmother no longer knew her, but that didn't mean she would give up on her. Not like so many others.

Chapter Ten

There is a disappearing act that follows Alzheimer's. As the brain of the patient begins its dissention into loss of time and space, friends of the afflicted also begin to disappear from giving their time and space. In Margaret's case it is as if folks forgot every card and/or letter she ever sent them; trips made to visit them, phone calls made to check in with them, and her welcome of their unexpected stop into her home were lost on them. This disease becomes a disease to all. People are uncomfortable sitting with someone who does not know them yet used to. We are caring and polite to strangers all day long, exchanging pleasantries because we need something from them, like our coffee. We make each other feel comfortable. We do this with and for strangers. We're polite. Yet when Alzheimer's strikes we seem to lose our manners and our compassion.

When I was a young child, we often went to visit Aunt Kitty. I don't know what was wrong with Aunt Kitty, but she was so old that she had seen Senator Abraham Lincoln on his train campaign. She was my father's aunt, and she had an attendant. She was bedridden. Her high bed sat in the center of the room, with its brass headboard and brass footboard holding on to her small body, while she was lost in it, covered in several quilts of faded reds and blues. She would usually be propped up by six or more starched white pillows, embracing her oddly colored darkened hair with hints of gray at its roots, piled on top off her head in an awkward, messy bun. Entering her bedroom from the light of day, my eyes would have to adjust to her darkened room. We entered, and we could only see her from the light of one or more lamps giving off muted light as their shades were covered by draped scarfs laid carefully over each. She and her room smelled of antiseptic, rose water, and urine—all but the latter in bottles and jars among many of various sizes and shapes, sitting atop a large doily-covered bedside table along with a water pitcher, several lipstick-stained glasses, and a framed drawing that she would call a picture of Lincoln at the back of a train. Every visit we would hear the story of her meeting Lincoln. I would ask Mom when we left almost as many times as Kitty told the story if it was true. Margaret would always say, "I have no idea, but just go along with it." It was never pleasant in that room. What was pleasant was Margaret's attitude.

Margaret was an angel to her aunts, my great-aunts. We only visited Aunt Kitty on my father's side, but there were two or three others on her side. I found these visits unpleasant, but watching Margaret interact with these women was fascinating. They seemed sort of crazy to me, telling the same stories over and over again. We would listen to each story each time. Sometimes cookies and teas distracted and pacified me. Some visits occurred inside in the case of Kitty, some on the porch in the case of Aunt Lottie, Mary's sister. It was usually just Mother and me that made these trips, and we did not make them often as Margaret didn't have a car until I was eleven years old. Bus trips were long and not easy during the seasons with snow, ice, and slush. I usually had something on my lap to protect, a casserole, a cake, or a pie that Mom had made from a recipe cut from a magazine. We would also take magazines and sometimes something extra like a pretty hankie or scarf.

It was during one of these trips when Mom and I were caught in a downpour that forced her to pull the car over to the side of the road and wait for the rain to lighten up. The rain was coming down in sheets that were both hard and heavy, pounding on the roof. There was little if any visibility. I was scared, and I knew she sensed that, although I said nothing. She was nervous. Margaret was always nervous, but she didn't want me to be scared, so she asked me if I wanted to pretend to drive. We struggled to trade seats, and she began to tell me where we were going, how long it would take, and how to get there. I had my small hands on the big steering wheel, with my legs tucked under my bottom to make me a bit higher in the seat. I had sat in our driveway many times and pretended to drive, so this was nothing new; however, this time Mom and I were going on a trip. I was driving, and she began to look at fake scenery, telling me of all she was seeing, while I was to keep my eyes on the road.

The water on the side of the road was beginning to rise rapidly, filling the trench that lay between us and the wire fencing that had run alongside us for miles. Cars had passed us and then pulled over in front of us. Cars had stopped behind us. There was no way to see how many, but she kept watch and would say in between spotting an invisible horse or cow, "I wonder if we should leave our lights on or off—"

When she asked this question, there was a profound silence that lingered in that car that meant something to each of us. We had sat there awaiting our fate, helpless in the hands of God—two prayers who did not pray but only waited. As the rain slowed and cars began to move past us, she pulled us back onto the road; she reached for the car light to pull them on, turning to smile at me as she did. That silence still lingered with us, and I felt changed.

I know how much it has cost to have my mother in the best of possible of situations. Having said that, I had not thought seriously about long-term health care for myself, that is not until Brenda was diagnosed with Alzheimer's. Brenda has lived comfortably alone for a long time, never remarried, working her job and having very little social time. She is a hoarder. She blocked most all family and most friends from entry to her home. A woman who used to love to entertain in her home no longer allowed most folks in. There is some school of thought that hoarding is a distant relative of Alzheimer's. It's a chicken-and-egg thought, but some connection is the idea. Margaret's basement grew to look like a hoarding situation, but I never thought of it that way. Brenda would not allow me to visit for a decade. Her daughter, Wendy, did not want to stay there and often chose a hotel over the situation at her mother's condo. Our cousin wanted to stay there and would insist in order to keep tabs on Brenda's mental health and ultimately her physical safety. My daughter stayed there and confirmed what we all feared—that it was indeed a bad situation. But Brenda just said she needed more room. She made weekly trips to The Salvation Army to shop. I hear tell that this meant more and more need for storage. Every wall was lined with storage baskets—floor to ceiling, corner to corner. She no longer could sleep in her bed as it was covered as well as surrounded with baskets. Clothes in various sizes were coming out of her closet, so racks had to be added outside its doors and around the room. A rack added to her shower kept her from showers, but there was no problem finding a toothbrush as dozens of them sat on and around her bathroom sink. Her cleaning lady finally stopped coming as there was no clear space left to clean. She had only been feather-dusting as it was. Piles of newspapers, magazines, flyers, and books lined all the hallways, two rows or more thick. Paramedics could not have gotten her out. Her only clear space became the sofa, which had become her bed.

This is the condition her space was in when she was taken into the hospital after she was found searching for her lost car in a parking lot. The police were called by a restaurant owner when Brenda ordered the same food for the third time within an hour without any money to pay for the third order. It was the hottest day of summer so far in Chicago. She was found by the police, sitting on a curb, complaining of how cold she was. She told them she couldn't find her purse or her car. Her purse was later found at the Big Lots store at the opposite end of where the restaurant was located. The police called the paramedics. She was taken in and not long after transferred to the third-floor psyche ward. This is where I first spoke with her as she sat in a hallway on a folding chair on a unit telephone. The nurse who had initially answered my call informed me that Brenda was doing well, but was very emotional and that she had a UTI that she was being treated for. After she recovered from that, she would be retested for Alzheimer's, although the thought was the results would be the same. My sister had our mother's disease.

Brenda was mad as hell. She had herself convinced that her children had conspired to get her in this situation. After the nurse put her on the phone, I pictured the actor Jack Nicholson walking by as my sister flew over the cuckoo's nest. As the week progressed, we learned that she would not be released unless and until family came to get her and took her to a facility. In other words she would not be going back home to her actual cuckoo's nest. Her son flew in to see her; her daughter, Wendy flew in to retrieve her. Wendy was told to not stop to collect her Mother's things, but to go directly to the airport and get her to the place that had been set up for her in California. This may have been a mistake as Brenda needed to collect herself, but the fear was if they went to her home without help, Wendy would never get her out again. My sister now lived in my state of California, something that we had spoken of for decades. But it wasn't going to be what I had dreamed of. We would not be hanging out or traveling or shopping or even eating out. For one thing she was in Northern California, and I was in Southern California. For another she was much worse than I had known anything about. I had seen the signs many times—the forgetfulness that isn't normal aging and/or stress-related. Brenda and I shared guilt over our mother's situation. I had given serious thought after Hal died to moving Mom out to California if I could. Brenda had given thought to moving her to Chicago. The timing never seemed right. I was not comfortable taking Mom away from all that she still knew. My brothers were there with their wives. My mom's siblings were all there. It was her state; her life was there in Ohio. Her disease was moving faster along than I could think things through. I knew it would be selfish of me to take her away. At the same time I knew I would spend every day with her. So we visited. I knew that it would help my siblings in Ohio if Brenda and I took turns to visit, thereby giving some relief to my brothers and their families. I often mentioned that, but Brenda always wanted to go when I went and never wanted to go when I didn't. It took me a long time to catch onto what was going on.

Our family had had quite a blowup over Mom. When one is dealing with this disease, this happens. Everyone has different opinions, and emotions run high. Most of us were not living inside the same world that Mom now lived in. We each felt she deserved better, but our views on what better meant varied. While I always tried to meet Mom where she was on a daily basis, others tried to make her remember, and others still tried to make her respond to us as she always had in our lives. After this *blowup* I was not interested in being anywhere but as close as I could be to Mom on my visits to Ohio, and Brenda was not interested in being anywhere but close to me. I thought at the time this had to do with family issues as it did with me. It didn't.

I booked a room within the facility where Mom stayed for an extended stay, and Brenda joined me. It was across the street from the Alzheimer's unit, not a far walk or a complicated one. The first day as Brenda and I unpacked, she looked for over an hour for several items that she had neglected to pack but sworn she had. I thought it odd at the time, but I've been known to forget to pack something. Each day that we were there, we arose to go feed Mom breakfast, and each day as Brenda took more and more time to get out the door, I became more and more aware of how disorganized she was. We walked the same hallway, the same stairs, the same lobby exit, the same street crossing, the same entrance to Mom's every day, and every day Brenda could not manage it on her own. At one point after I had left Brenda and our mother alone to go get some coffee drinks, I received a call on my cell from security.

"Is this Christie?"

"Yes," I said.

"This is security over here at the . . . where your Mom is, and your sister, Brenda, is here. She asked me to call you. She's very upset, not sure where you are and not sure where she is staying or how to get there."

I was horrified. I had only been gone about fifteen minutes.

The next time that I knew my beautiful, full-of-life, funny and spontaneous sister was headed down a path of lost memories and lost confidence was on a trip arranged for her, myself, my daughter, and Wendy to Las Vegas.

We had a lovely rented condo, tickets to some shows, and plans for sightseeing. It was the first night, and we were headed out for dinner and a show. The condo was on the second floor with a nice view overlooking the pool and the lush palm-covered grounds below. When you walked in the front door, the first thing you notice are the sliding glass doors that led to a small patio with a table and four chairs and the view. There was a sofa just past the small kitchen with a small bar overlooking a table and chairs. Across from the sofa was a wall unit with stereo and television. Just past the wall unit was a door that lead to one of the two bedrooms. As we got ready to leave, I opened the only door leading out of the condo to the hall, the very same one that we had entered from. Lacey went out the door. Wendy went out the door, and Brenda stopped, looked around, and said, "This isn't the way out."

I said, "Yep, it is. Let's go."

She paused, looked around, and said that this was not the way we had come in and there had to be another way. Wendy came back in and said, "This is why it's time for meds, Mom." Unaware that there had been this talk between mother and daughter, I just froze. Brenda continued to look bewildered, while Wendy continued to speak of medication. Lacey was already at the stairs. I walked over and offered Brenda my arm. I told her that if she would like to search for another way out, I would be happy to join her in her search, but I knew the way out and we could leave straight away if she wanted to come my way. In my opinion that is how you join a person right where they are.

We went onto to enjoy one of the best evenings of my life. The show was Chippendales male dance review. Upon our arrival Brenda secured herself a seat front and center, with her chair facing the stage. She put on her glasses and told us not to speak to her until after the show, and she was dead serious! Lacey giggled out loud through the whole show, which made me giggle. Poor Wendy acted like she didn't know any of us, actually leaving our table. It was hilarious. This is my sister—fun, cooperative, carefree, and disorganized. She is also insecure, self-centered, compassionate, and highly emotional. How exactly she can be all of those things has always amazed me. She has found herself in a very difficult situation, yet with all of the anger and fear that she feels, she will handle this with humor, self-preservation, and grace. I will watch as her daughter and her son make mistakes that I will try to prevent, and I will give advice both sought and not solicited. I will pray that they will listen and find the way to join their mother in her world as she slowly slips out of ours, for that is the only way to love unconditionally a person with Alzheimer's.

Chapter Eleven

During the last years of Margaret's life I spent countless hours in the Alzheimer's unit. It is a comfortable, secluded, lovely place with lovely personnel. The patients are all different: mean, nice, scared, smart, unable to speak, hard to get along with, very easygoing, cantankerous, loud, quiet, talented, narcissistic, compassionate, healthy, sickly and of course all shapes and sizes. Every once in a while there would be someone who didn't last long working there because of their lack of understanding of the world in which these folks now lived. Like a volunteer who told Edna, a very quiet, wondering woman who had lost her husband years before, that her husband was dead and not coming to see her today. Edna didn't remember that, so each time someone reminded her, she had to grieve again. Or there was another volunteer who brought Martha to her room and told her to stay put and not to come out until she was told she could, as if the woman was five years old. These folks are not children, and they are not undeserving of our respect. They have lived long, productive lives. They have personalities that we may like or dislike. They may be strong-willed. They may be meek. They may be angry, sad, scared, lonely, or ready for a party. Their Alzheimer's has not changed who they are. They have not lost their pride, and their dignity is still important to them and should be to us. I used to watch a woman walk around the living area of the main room while I sat with my mom. She was tall, and she was always asking about her gloves. That's all she ever said to anyone. The living area was large but crowded with a full seven-foot sofa on the back wall and one in the front facing the TV. Overstuffed chairs lined the other walls, and a piano sat in the corner. Those who could not walk, which eventually became Mom, filled in any and all empty spaces with their wheelchairs. This tall woman would walk constantly around, bending over to pick up any little thing that was on the floor, ranging from a dirty tissue or napkin to the tiniest piece of lint. She would sometimes stop and stare at me or others and asked about her gloves. I made the assumption as did others that she meant warm gloves, but then we all decided that maybe these were dress gloves as she was from a time when one wore such gloves. One day I happen to catch her husband on a visit. I struck up a conversation and mentioned the glove thing. He said that it was probably garden gloves as she had gardened and had been obsessed with weeds. Bingo. Not only had we just solved the glove issue, but we also found out why she risked her back health by her constant bending to pick up every piece of floor litter. It was because of *weeds*!

There is always a reason for the why and the how of an Alzheimer's patient's behaviors and habits. Always. You and I may not know it because we cannot know every detail of one's life, but nothing is random or crazy. This is not a crazy disease. It is a disease of one's life as they have known it and as we have known it. Like music that has been proven to help folks with their anxiety, understanding that their little idiosyncrasies are not little at all but confused memory of activities and habits that they hold dear can go a long way in saving quality of life for them. Wouldn't it be lovely if she were out in a garden and doing what she wanted to be doing? That said, in her mind she is doing it, so let us not stop her or make assumptions about her behavior. The end of one's mind and/or life is often a time of assumption for many of us. It's easier. After all the end of one's mind seems to most of us like the end of life. But is it? This is what my family and I spent lots of time talking about. The doctor that Brenda, Donna, and I requested to meet with presumed that we only asked to meet with him and end her various drug therapies so as to end her life. I don't blame him for thinking that, but I do hold him accountable for his lack of bedside manner with us, the patients of the disease as much, if not more than the patient herself. After a certain point in time every person who loves a person with Alzheimer's becomes somewhat of a patient even if it is only the need to attend to our own depression over this state of illness. My own depression lifted only after my mother's death. Once I could grieve not only over her passing but over her loss of memory, then and only then did I leave her world, which I had entered without a door back out. I knew intuitively from very early on with the discovery of Margaret's fate that I would meet her with every visit right where she was. I went to greet her always with a toothy smile, never argued with her tenuous state or her tenacious personality. I accepted her disease with as much bravery as I could muster. I became depressed because I made the mistake of not leaving her Alzheimer's at her door, but carried it into mine. I was not my Mother's care-giver; I could have visited, been my best self while with her and left my sadness in the Alzheimer's unit. That said there was no time for sadness. I had to be joyful, attentive and selfless when I was with her. When I left her I wanted to be happy and grateful for my life with my family and friends. The trick and/or the balance of Alzheimer's is keeping your sense of humor. It is all that will get you through and all that will get them through as healthy as possible. I am working on not making that mistake again. While I visit with my sister, we will acknowledge over and over again that there is a dis–ease that has come once again into our lives. We have vowed to keep laughing. Brenda is a different person. I am a different person. Margaret was brave as she had been her whole life in this last decade of lost memory. She never lost her mind, her spirit, or her heart. She held on to kindness as best as she could in a time of great fear, never losing sight of her commitment to herself to be brave in the face of any danger, any betrayal, or any loss.

Mother's Day of 2002 I made a decision to do something for myself that I felt would serve me well in the times ahead with my mom. I wanted to spend alone time with my sister and my mom. I had never had that in my life. I booked a motel suite, and I made plans to meet up with Brenda and whisked Mom away from Hal for a girl's trip. We surprised her one morning while she was still in bed. Hal, a bit of a chauvinist, was none too happy about it. We had the time of our lives: room service, shopping, movies, coffee stops and chats, laughs and lots of love filled our few days. Mom said over and over again that she would never forget it. I made a scrapbook of our adventure to help her maintain the memory for as long as possible. Even after she could no longer remember it, she would see that book and pull it out to show people. It remains one of the best things that I ever did for myself.

Margaret Francis West Larason Wright lived to be ninety years old. She was under the care of hospice for the last four years of her life. Her sister, Mildred, had passed a year before, her mind healthy. Her sister, Dorothy, is having memories issues, and her brother, Joe, has dementia. Lacey divorced, and now she is engaged. She and her fiancé, Ben, got to visit Mom shortly before she passed, and for that I am so grateful. Tom and Donna were on a road trip, part of which was a visit to see Mark and me the week that Margaret took her last breath. They had arrived back in Ohio in time for Tom to be with her at her bedside. I thought that by the end of this writing I may know why my mother had to have this disease the last decade of her life and perhaps longer, for we are not sure when it started. I do not know. She experienced all the suspected things that have been associated with Alzheimer's, including using products with aluminum on her body and in her cookware. Her diet also is suspect since it, too, included foods suspected of causing this disease. What I do know is that a woman lived to bear great suffering and that at times it was too much for her. She was angry at a man who also suffered from disease. She never forgave him, although she did try to be compassionate toward him near the end of his days on this earth. He left her with great pain, which rendered her hopeless at many times in her life. She married well but carried jealousy within her bones, jealousy borne from fear of leftover betrayal. She had great fear of loss, and although she was a woman of faith, that faith was not of or in herself. I believe that she abandoned herself because that felt safer than ending up alone in a field of tall weeds, knowing that fear was all around her. She had been brave for all her life, and she could be brave through this too. What I did was stand beside her. I couldn't change her or talk her out of fear, loss, anger, or abandonment issues. I could only do what she had taught me: be kind, be brave, be compassionate, and when people need you, be there for them as long as you can in any way that you can. She walked me down the aisle and helped me lay down soft petals for the path that my sister was about to take, and now I can do that on my own. As of today I no longer suffer with anxiety. I live in the present moment, and my mind, my memory and my heart are perfect, whole, and complete. I am my mother, and that is a blessing. I am just not taking her road.

Thank you Mark my love, for seeing me through it all. This is my story of how I remember both my mother and how we affected each other's lives. My family members all have their own stories. I want to thank them all, alive and those who have passed on, for their love and caring of a woman who loved and cared for us all.